The CIA

WORLD ESPIONAGE

❖❖❖❖❖❖❖❖❖❖❖❖❖❖

The CIA

Graham Yost

Facts On File
New York • Oxford

The CIA

> Facts On File
> 460 Park Avenue South
> New York, New York 10016

Library of Congress Cataloging-in-Publication Data

Yost, Graham.
    The CIA / Graham Yost.
      p. cm. — (World espionage)
    Includes index.
    Summary: Traces the history of the Central Intelligence Agency,
examining its covert operations at home and abroad.
    ISBN 0-8160-1941-X
    1. United States.   Central Intelligence Agency—Juvenile
literature. [1. United States.   Central Intelligence Agency.
2. Spies.   3. United States—Foreign relations—1945-] I. Title.
II. Series.
JK468.I6Y67 1989
327.1'2'06073—dc19   88-25190

British CIP data available on request

Printed in the United States of America

10 9 8 7 6 5 4 3 2 1

CONTENTS

Stalin was advised, time and again, not to trust Hitler, but he ignored such talk. He could ignore it no longer when, on June 22, 1941, Hitler took his campaign eastward into the Soviet Union.

The United States had been supporting the British with arms and other materials from the beginning of the war, but there was great resistance in America to sending U.S. troops into the fray. That resistance ended on December 7, 1941, when Japanese forces attacked the U.S. Navy base at Pearl Harbor in Hawaii. Japan, like Germany, had its own dreams of empire, one encompassing the Pacific Ocean. Because Japan had joined the Axis powers, when the United States entered the war against Japan, it also got into the fight in Europe.

In World War II, the United States and the Soviet Union, the two great enemies of the postwar era, were actually allies, fighting together against a common enemy. When the war ended, that bond quickly dissolved.

There had long been a certain amount of tension between the two nations, caused by strong ideological differences. The fight between the Americans and the Soviets is social, economic and political. It's not just a matter of Western democracy (the people elect leaders to represent them) versus Soviet totalitarianism (one party rules the state, and the state controls everything). It's also a matter of capitalism (U.S. industry is owned privately and run for profit) versus communism (all Soviet industry is owned collectively by the people and all income is shared). While these differences were put aside during World War II, they surfaced again quickly and became even more pronounced in the postwar years.

One reason the tension grew between these two nations is that the stakes increased. When the United States dropped atomic bombs on Hiroshima and Nagasaki, two Japanese cities, to end the war with Japan in August 1945, a new era, the nuclear era, began for the planet. And when the Soviets joined the nuclear club by detonating their first bomb in 1949, nations possessed the means to wage total war for the first time—war that could annihilate the planet.

1
SETTING THE SCENE

In the 1930s, Adolf Hitler led his National Socialist, or Nazi, Party into power in Germany. Hitler's ideas and those of Nazism were characterized by a belief in the need for totalitarian or fascist government—that is, that all aspects of life are to be overseen and controlled by the government—and in a belief that all who didn't fit the Nazis' racial mold, especially Jews, should be exterminated. Hitler and the Nazis also believed that their will should prevail, not only throughout Germany but over all of Europe as well.

By the end of the decade, Hitler had begun his expansion and in 1939 German troops crossed into Poland. In response to this act of aggression, Britain declared war on Germany. The sides quickly took shape, with Germany and Italy, the Axis powers, on one side, and Britain and a handful of other countries, the Allies, on the other side.

Neither the Soviet Union nor the United States was involved in the beginning of the war. The Soviets, led by the tyrannical Josef Stalin, had signed a nonaggression pact—we won't attack you and you won't attack us—with Germany.

and one American. Soviet spies work for their Committee for State Security—the KGB, an institution that is covered in another volume in this series. This book is about the American soldiers of the Cold War, the people who work for the Central Intelligence Agency—the CIA.

As horrendous a threat as they are, nuclear weapons have, in a perverse way, contributed to a kind of peace, for both sides are afraid of risking a large-scale war, knowing the possible consequences.

But war has gone on; it has just been fought by different means. It has been fought—on and off—but mostly on for the past four decades, and it has been played out all around the world. The United States and the Soviet Union are the "superpowers," for they are the nuclear powers and, hence, the most powerful. The other countries in the world have been asked to choose sides. For many, especially among the industrialized nations, the choice was automatic. On the side of the Soviets are the Eastern bloc nations, such as Hungary, Poland and Czechoslovakia, which the Soviets took control of after World War II. On the American side are Canada, Australia, Japan and the noncommunist countries of Europe. But for many countries, the poorer countries that make up what is known as the Third World, the choice has not been easy. It has been in those countries, in Africa, Central and South America and Asia, that the struggle for control between the Soviets and the Americans—the Cold War—has been fought the hardest.

It's called the Cold War because, unlike "hot" wars, it involves no troops, guns or airplanes. The Cold War between the superpowers has been fought without soldiers and without tanks. Instead, it has been fought by diplomats and politicians, who seek to gain favor and influence in the countries they wish to bring into their camp. That's all aboveboard, something we see on the news, when the U.S. secretary of state or the Soviet foreign minister are seen shaking hands in some foreign capital.

But there is another way the Cold War is fought, and it's not something we see on the news. It doesn't take place in the light of day. It takes place in shadows, under cover; and the people trying to influence the course of events aren't diplomats, they're spies.

Every country has its spy agency, but just as there are two superpowers, so there are two major spy services, one Soviet

The Intelligence Community

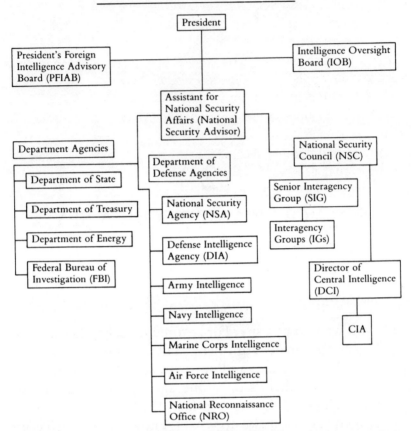

Although the CIA was created to coordinate all U.S. intelligence gathering activities, it doesn't actually work that way. The other intelligence agencies—the departmental agencies and the Department of Defense agencies—report to the President through his Assistant for National Security Affairs (the National Security Advisor). The CIA operates under the watchful eye of the National Security Council, which is composed of the President, the Vice-President, the Secretary of State and the Secretary of Defense. The DCI does exert some control over the other agencies through the Senior Interagency Group (SIG), which is composed of the DCI, National Security Advisor, the Deputy Secretaries of State and Defense, the Deputy Attorney General, the Director of the FBI and the Director of the NSA. The Interagency Groups (IGs) are smaller groups that deal with specific interagency matters. The President's Foreign Intelligence Advisory Board (PFIAB) is a nongovernmental body, appointed by the President to advise him on the future course of intelligence. The Intelligence Oversight Board (IOB) is a permanent, nonpartisan (that is, both Democrats and Republicans are on the board) group that examines intelligence activities in terms of questions of constitutional legality.

2

SO, YOU WANT TO BE A SPY

Do you want to be a spy? For argument's sake, let's say that you do, and for further argument's sake, let's say you want to spy *for* the United States and not against it. If that's the case, you might think there's only one agency to work for, the Central Intelligence Agency. In fact, the CIA is only one of several agencies that make up what is known as the *intelligence community* of the United States. Besides the CIA there is the National Security Agency (NSA), responsible for intercepting the communications of other nations and breaking their codes; the National Reconnaissance Office (NRO), part of Air Force intelligence, responsible for operating America's spy satellites; separate army and navy intelligence services; the Defense Intelligence Agency, which coordinates the work of the service intelligence agencies; and a handful of smaller agencies (even the Treasury Department has an intelligence wing).

But the CIA does remain *the* intelligence agency. It may not have the biggest budget—that honor goes to either the NSA or the NRO, both of which are at least three times the size of

Arlington, Virginia. Here CTs are given instruction in the importance of security, the organization of the agency and intelligence community and the overall goals of the CIA. Next, they are sent to the "Farm," a base outside of Williamsburg, Virginia, which is disguised as a Pentagon research and testing facility. There, CTs are shown training films and given light-weapons training. They receive instruction in basic espionage techniques—such as how to plant a bug, tail a suspect, interrogate and so on. Every CT gets this training even though most officers will never use any of these techniques in their work. If, however, they are bound for possible paramilitary work, then they will get further training—in sabotage, nighttime parachute jumps and the like. Graduate training in this line is given at Fort Bragg, North Carolina, and special jungle training is provided at Fort Gulick in Panama.

Once your first year of formal training is completed, your on-the-job training begins. Where you spend your year of on-the-job training depends on what assignment you and the agency have chosen. The CIA is divided into four main sections, called directorates. If you want to be a spy, you can forget two of these four: the Directorate of Science and Technology and the Directorate of Administration. The Directorate of Science and Technology has two functions. It reviews intelligence of a scientific nature—for example, what the latest Soviet advances in particle beam weaponry are, and it looks at ways science and technology can be used in spying, such as in the use of spy satellites. The Directorate of Administration is responsible for personnel, training, finance and security. If you want to be a spy you'll be thinking of either the Directorate of Intelligence or the Directorate of Operations.

The Intelligence Directorate doesn't do the most glamorous work, but it does do some of the most important. This is where analysts toil, trying to figure what the importance is of Agent X's report from Czechoslovakia that there is a deep schism in the Soviet leadership and what effect the failed wheat crop in the Urals will have on Soviet leader Michail Gorbachev's economic restructuring. The National

the CIA in terms of budget and manpower. It may not have the coordinating power over the intelligence community that the name *Central* implies. Even so, it's the CIA one thinks of when one thinks of America and spying.

If you want to join the CIA, you're not alone—many, many more people apply to join the agency than are accepted. What kind of person is the CIA looking for? In the fifties and sixties, most CIA recruits were graduates of Ivy League schools (there was a special preponderance of Yale men, particularly those who had belonged to Skull and Bones, a secret society). But now that the Ivy League students are being pulled into ever higher paying jobs in business, the CIA recruiters are turning to less prestigious private universities and state schools. They are still looking for the same basic attribute in a prospective employee that they always have—intelligence.

Despite what one may think of the various exploits of the CIA over the years, it has not been run by dumb people. One of the most important figures in CIA history, Richard Bissell, was a professor of economics at MIT before he joined the agency; Stansfield Turner, the director of central intelligence (the top spot) under President Jimmy Carter, was a Rhodes scholar. While a background in political science and Russian studies might help, agency recruiters are generally impressed by excellence in most any field. Fluency in another language and a facility for learning other languages is extremely important.

If you were recruited by the CIA and you accepted, you'd then become a career trainee. For the most part, the only entry into the agency is through the bottom—you enter there as an officer and rise up through the ranks. The only exceptions to this are in highly technical fields where an expert might be brought in at a high level; and in the upper ranks—such as director, deputy director and the heads of the various directorates—where people are sometimes brought in from outside.

Career trainees—CTs for short—go through a two-year training period. The first year is spent in formal training; the second year is on-the-job training. Formal training usually begins with introductory courses at the Broyhill Building in

Photographic Interpretation Center is also a part of this directorate. It is responsible for analyzing the spy pictures taken by satellites and planes.

The Directorate of Operations is known in the agency, rather straightforwardly, as *Clandestine Services*. This is the directorate that has made the CIA famous—or infamous—around the world. It is divided roughly into three areas: espionage, counterespionage and covert action.

Espionage is classic spying—penetrating foreign governments with agents or recruiting spies from the other side. While some countries around the world have been infiltrated by CIA agents, the greatest effort is put into trying to recruit people already working in the other governments. This is especially true when it comes to countries such as the Soviet Union and China which, because of their ever-present and efficient internal security forces, are almost impossible to penetrate with American agents. Most CIA officers who recruit foreign spies work under the cover of the U.S. embassy.

What do these officers do? Well, there are several basic steps to recruiting a spy. The prospective spy must first be *spotted*—identified as a foreign national who seems willing to spy—then *evaluated*: Will he (or she) be worth it, and can he be trusted? The actual *recruiting* will be done by a CIA outsider, brought in so that there will be no connection between the spotter and the agency—if the whole thing blows up, the spotter's cover won't be harmed.

Once they sign on, prospective spies are *tested* to see how good their information is—they will usually be asked for something the agency already has so that its validity can be checked. Then, if a new agent passes the test and needs it, he or she will be *trained* in the basic techniques of spy tradecraft—how to make contact, pass messages, take clandestine photos, avoid being followed and other techniques. Then, the agent must be *handled*. To *handle* an agent means to do anything and everything that must be done to keep that recruit spying. Some agents require more handling than others: Oleg

Central Intelligence Agency

We're looking for you special men and women who still have a spirit of adventure.

There aren't many of you. One in a thousand, maybe. You're a bright, self-reliant, self-motivated person we need to help us gather information and put together a meaningful picture of what's happening in the world. One of an elite corps of men and women.

You can rely on your wits, your initiative, and your skills. And, in return, enjoy recognition, positions of responsibility, life in foreign places, plus knowing that you belong to a small, very special group of people doing a vital, meaningful job in the face of challenges and possible hardship.

You'd gain valuable experience because the opportunity we offer would give you the chance to develop your ability to take charge, make decisions, use your imagination, be creative, and work with others.

Among the qualifications. a college education, U.S. citizenship, foreign language aptitude.

If all this sounds too good to be true, you owe yourself a closer look. Send your résumé in confidence to

Personnel Representative
Dept. A, Room 821
P.O. Box 1925
Washington, D.C. 20013

No obligation, and we'll keep your inquiry confidential.

CENTRAL INTELLIGENCE AGENCY

It's time for us to know more about each other.

An equal-opportunity affirmative-action employer.

Do you want to be a spy? This CIA employment opportunities ad appeared in the Washington Post in 1979. [Credit: UPI/Bettmann Newsphotos]

overthrow of the government of Guatemala through the Bay of Pigs invasion to the current contra versus Sandinista battle in Nicaragua have been run by the covert action wing.

Whatever directorate you work for, and whether you work out of an embassy in Bahrain or in the agency's huge headquarters in Langley, Virginia, you will be working for the same company, and in the same atmosphere. The overriding characteristic of this atmosphere is secrecy. The words over the main entrance may be "And ye shall know the truth and the truth shall make you free," but their meaning to the CIA is finding out the truth about other nations, not anyone finding out the truth about the CIA.

There are rigorous security precautions at the agency. For a long time the sign on the road into the agency's headquarters identified it as a Bureau of Public Roads facility. Just so that no one can get a complete rundown of who works for the agency, not everyone's name appears in the agency phone book; the book is changed every six months, with new names being

An aerial shot of CIA headquarters in Langley, Virginia, a suburb of Washington, D.C. [Credit: Courtesy of the Central Intelligence Agency]

Penkovsky, who was an invaluable source in Moscow in the late fifties and early sixties, loved America and so, to keep him happy, was given "secret" American citizenship (something, tragically, he never got to exercise). Finally, once the operation is over, the agent must be *terminated*. That's not as dire as it sounds. It usually means making sure the agent is reasonably happy and will not betray the operation; sometimes this involves spiriting the agent out of his country to safety and a new life in the United States, Canada or Latin America.

Espionage is a rather complex and involved business, yet it pales in comparison to *counterespionage*—the work of stopping the other side's agents, which is the most intricate arena of spying. It's the gritty world of spy versus spy, with one side trying to outwit the other with ever more wild and complicated deceptions. The CIs, as counterespionage experts are known, learn to suspect everyone and everything. It is the CI's job to protect the CIA from being infiltrated by foreign agents (it is the FBI's job, in general, to stop foreign intelligence gathering in the United States).

As far as anyone knows, the CIs have been successful. The CIA—unlike the British intelligence services, which have been riddled with Soviet agents in high places—has never been penetrated at a high level by the KGB. Some feel this is because the CIs are so good at their job. The CIs don't necessarily accept the compliment—they assume that the KGB has managed such a penetration, but that it has been so clever that no one has been able to spot it. It is such unrelenting suspicion that has led people in other parts of the agency to feel that the CIs have, on occasion, crossed over into the land of the certifiably paranoid.

It's the covert action officers of Clandestine Services that achieve the most notoriety, though. These are the fellows who try to sway the elections in other countries, who have resorted to outright sabotage, who have come up with the assorted "dirty tricks" spy paraphernalia—everything from poison pens to exploding seashells—that rivals the stuff shown in James Bond films. Operations from the 1954

removed and others being replaced. Security guards watch the cleaning staff each night; indeed, in some areas an officer must be present. If you want to advertise a car for sale on a bulletin board, you're only allowed to leave your first name and phone extension. And, until the early 1970s, if you met someone at a party and were asked where you worked, you were supposed to lie and say, "the State Department," or "Defense." If a senior officer has to have surgery, there will often be a security officer in the operating room to see if the officer says anything while under anesthesia.

But the CIA rewards and encourages this secrecy by taking very good care of its employees, who, with the notable exception of a few whistle-blowers, return this care with great loyalty. The idea is for the CIA to take care of all an employee's needs. The agency credit union will give you a loan; the agency will arrange for health, home and auto insurance; there's an employee activity association that sets up baseball leagues, picnics and classes in karate and pottery. There's a travel agency and a theater ticket service. If you want to further your education, the agency will even arrange for its own officers to teach college-level courses for which you'll be given credit at a local university. If you get sick, you can go to an in-house doctor or an outside one who has been cleared by the agency. If you have a drinking problem, the agency will help you with it. It will even provide for the services of a psychiatrist (given the nature of the work, mental breakdowns are fairly common and don't carry much of a stigma).

Sound good? Before you decide whether or not you want to give Langley a call, you should know a little bit of the history of the CIA, and what it has been up to since it came into being shortly after the end of World War II.

CIA Organization

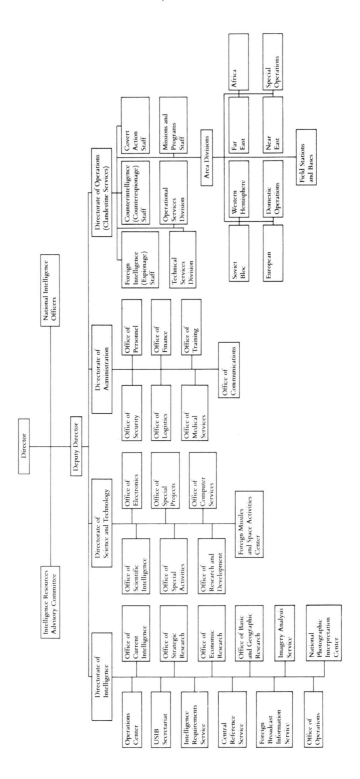

The creation of the CIG, and later the CIA, was not undertaken lightly, and its birth was not an easy one. There were many—Truman among them—who were made uneasy by the idea of America having any spy agency at all during peacetime. It conjured up an image of "secret police," something that doesn't jibe too well with the notions of liberty and democracy. Others, however, argued that if you wait until war before you spy, you've waited too long; in fact, having a good intelligence operation—knowing what the other side is up to—is perhaps the best defense against a war's occurring in the first place.

The most outspoken supporter of peacetime spying, indeed the true father of centralized intelligence in the United States, was William "Wild Bill" Donovan, the man who headed up the nation's wartime house of spies, the Office of Strategic Services (OSS).

Well before America was drawn into the war with the Japanese bombing of Pearl Harbor in 1941, as war engulfed Europe, President Franklin Delano Roosevelt recognized the need for intelligence gathering. When he looked for someone to start up an infant intelligence operation, Donovan was the perfect choice.

Donovan received his nickname "Wild Bill" from his buddies in World War I for his battlefield exploits and heroics. Like so many of the U.S. senior intelligence officers and spymasters that have followed him down the years, Donovan was a member in good standing of the Eastern establishment, moneyed and well connected in business and in government. By the time he came to Roosevelt's attention he was a millionaire, had been assistant attorney general and had made a run, albeit an unsuccessful one, on the Republican ticket for governor of New York in 1932. More important, his connections ran outside the United States. He was well traveled, was friendly with countless highly placed officials throughout Europe and was well respected in the countries that were soon to become, along with America, the Allies.

Immediately after Pearl Harbor, Donovan's small-time intelligence operation went big-time very quickly. It was given

3

OUT OF THE ASHES OF THE OSS

In the early part of 1946, President Harry S. Truman held a lunch for his Chief of Staff, Admiral Leahy, and another Navy veteran, Admiral Sidney Souers, in celebration of Souers's appointment as the first director of the newly formed Central Intelligence Group. At some point during the lunch, Truman handed out daggers, dark hats, cloaks and false mustaches to Leahy and Souers, asking them to "accept vestments and appurtenances of their respective positions, namely as Personal Snooper and Director of Centralized Snooping."

Truman was known for his sense of humor, and undoubtedly much of the reason he gave these men the objects most commonly associated with espionage—to this day spying is occasionally referred to as "cloak and dagger work"—was because he simply thought it funny. But it is also likely that there was an undercurrent to the joke, an undercurrent of worry. When Truman signed the directive dated January 22, 1946 that brought the Central Intelligence Group, the immediate forerunner of the CIA, into existence, he created America's first peacetime spy agency.

war were J. Edgar Hoover, head of the FBI, and the chiefs of the various services of the armed forces. They all saw a postwar OSS as a threat—something that would encroach on their areas of responsibility.

To thwart the plan, they raised the specter of "secret police." Hoover leaked a copy of Donovan's memo and Roosevelt's drafted executive order to *Chicago Tribune* reporter Walter J. Trohan. The resulting article, published February 9, 1945, touched off a storm of controversy over whether or not Roosevelt was planning on setting up an "American Gestapo." Any mention of America and Hitler's secret police in the same breath spelled disaster and the proposal was squashed.

Nevertheless, Donovan still had Roosevelt's support. But he lost the backing of the Oval Office when Roosevelt died—President Truman was wary of the idea. To make matters worse for Donovan, Truman's budget director was Harold Smith, someone Donovan had thoroughly antagonized during the war. It looked as if Donovan had lost his fight when, on October 1, 1945, Truman signed an order that broke up the OSS. Some parts were sent to the State and War departments while other parts simply ceased to exist. "Wild Bill" Donovan, the father of American intelligence, was out of a job. Though he never again served as America's spymaster, his influence on the course of American intelligence continues to be felt to this day.

It didn't take long for the problems caused by the breakup of the OSS to become apparent. Indeed, even before the October 1 decree, Secretary of the Navy James Forrestal thought that there might be trouble. In September 1945, he commissioned New York lawyer Ferdinand Eberstadt to draft a report on America's future intelligence needs. Eberstadt quickly saw that the biggest problem was that the left hand didn't know what the right hand was doing. Intelligence was being collected all over the place, but it wasn't being coordinated. The consequences could be serious—as Pearl Harbor had shown. Various intelligence sources had provided advance warning of the surprise Japanese attack before it

the name it's remembered by, the Office of Strategic Services, and its headquarters were moved to London. There Donovan worked closely with another William—William Stephenson—code name "Intrepid," a Canadian who was the liaison between U.S. and British intelligence. Wild Bill and Intrepid were a study in contrasts, the brazen American and the quiet Canadian, but they worked well together and they worked hard.

They coordinated many of the resistance movements (underground groups that fought against the Germans) throughout Europe, placed agents in the field from Cairo to Tokyo, sent teams on sabotage missions from Norway to Burma, and raised deception and disinformation to an art form. By the end of the war, the OSS had 13,000 employees and a budget of $37 million. But, by war's end, there were many who felt that there was no need to keep such an operation going. Donovan, obviously, was not one of them.

Donovan thought that an intelligence agency would be just as important for a nation at peace as for one at war. He and many others felt that while two of America's enemies, Germany and Japan, had been defeated, conflict with a third, the Soviet Union, an ally during the war, was looming on the horizon. Donovan didn't want the United States to be as ill-informed about the intentions of Russia as it had been about Germany and Japan.

Donovan sent a memo to Roosevelt in 1944, outlining what he felt would be America's peacetime intelligence needs, which, as he saw it, would require an organization not unlike the OSS, headed by someone not unlike himself. He believed that the talent should not be wasted. Roosevelt agreed with Donovan and drafted an executive order in support of the idea.

But Donovan had made a good number of enemies at home during the war. Though he got away with a certain amount of toe-trampling and feather-ruffling with the country locked in battle, he caused many people to resent the OSS and look forward to its termination at the end of the conflict. The people most incensed at the idea of the OSS living on past the

direct conflict with an old foe of Donovan's, the FBI. At that time the FBI ran all U.S. spying operations in Latin America. The CIG thought that this should fall under its jurisdiction, and after a heated political battle it won that right.

The next step involved expanding the group's power. On July 8, 1946, the CIG appeared before the National Intelligence Authority (NIA), the oversight committee. The CIG lobbied to expand the scope of the job of the director of central intelligence, giving the director the power to conduct all espionage and counterespionage activities outside the United States. When the NIA agreed to this it essentially negated its own role—the CIG was supposed to report to the NIA, but with these expanded powers it really didn't have to report to anyone but the president.

On went the expansion. The surviving bits of the OSS that had been scattered to the wind were brought back into the fold. Within one year the CIG had expanded to six times its original size. Perhaps the biggest accomplishment in that first year was to get Truman's full backing (indeed, by the end of his administration, Truman's first talk of the day was always with the DCI).

On September 18, 1947, the Central Intelligence *Group* became the Central Intelligence *Agency* with the passing of the National Security Act. This act also did away with the NIA, creating in its stead the National Security Council (NSC), to which the newly formed CIA would be answerable.

One of the questions posed during the congressional hearings held before the passing of the act concerned the size of the CIA—how big would it be. Future DCI Allen Dulles, an OSS veteran, testified that it should be small, for "if this thing gets to be a great big octopus it should not function well." How small? "Abroad you will need a certain number of people, but it ought not to be a great number. It ought to be scores rather than hundreds."

But of course it did not stay small. Indeed, a half-joking unofficial motto at the CIA in those first few months of its life was "Bigger than State by Forty-eight." And, sure enough, it wasn't long before the CIA was indeed bigger than the State

happened on December 7, 1941, but the information wasn't passed on to the right people at the right time. No one wanted another Pearl Harbor.

Truman heeded the advice. On January 22, 1946, he signed into being the Central Intelligence Group (CIG). He was still wary, however, because he saw the potential for the abuse of power. Nevertheless, he saw the need for a central clearinghouse for intelligence. What he did not intend, however, was for the CIG to be a continuation of the OSS. There were to be no covert operations (no OSS-style sabotage and subversion missions). Indeed, the CIG wasn't even supposed to gather its own intelligence—it was just supposed to bring the intelligence already gathered into one place, evaluate it, then distribute it. To make sure the CIG did only what it was supposed to, Truman also created an oversight group, the National Intelligence Authority, which consisted of the secretaries of the State Department, War Department and the Navy Department and Truman's own appointee.

The CIG then was a defanged, declawed version of the OSS. For OSS veterans it was better than nothing, but they weren't going to settle for it. It didn't take long for America's spy agency to get its fangs and claws back.

Admiral Souers, the nation's first director of central intelligence (DCI), got the ball rolling by organizing the CIG into a bureaucracy. It seems it's the nature of every bureaucracy to expand, and the CIG expanded, rapidly. Souers left after six months to move closer to the White House, becoming the president's assistant for intelligence affairs.

The man who succeeded Souers, Lieutenant General Hoyt S. Vandenberg, did even more to expand the CIG and consolidate its powers. When he was asked how he saw his job he replied, "I will tell you this; I do not believe in any damn coordinating sewing circle."

The first step was to get the claws back—to regain the power to collect intelligence instead of merely coordinating it, to spy for themselves instead of just reading other agencies' spy reports. The first part of this quest brought the CIG into

CONTENTS

Department. In the years 1947 to 1953, spurred on by fear of the Soviet Union, the CIA expanded another sixfold. In 1947, the CIA had a staff of 302 working in the United States and in its seven stations overseas at an annual cost of $4.7 million. By 1952 it had a staff of 2,812 working in 47 stations abroad with a budget of $82 million.

The early CIA was heavily populated with OSS veterans. They had seen to it that the CIG regained its claws—the power to collect intelligence. The next big step was to reclaim its fangs—the authority to conduct covert operations overseas. The OSS veterans weren't happy with just collecting information, they wanted to *make things happen.* These men had had the most exciting and rewarding time of their lives during the war. Working with resistance groups, subverting local governments, going on sabotage missions—this was truly heroic work. They missed it. And they felt it was the kind of work that could be done to great effect all around the world.

But, the question in 1947 was whether or not covert operations would have any place in America's intelligence agency. When then-Director Vandenberg testified before Congress, he said the CIA would merely collect and coordinate. There was no mention of covert work, despite the fact that earlier in the year some ex-OSS staffers in the CIG had already begun planning covert operations abroad.

At the heart of the CIA there was and is a split that divides the agency into two halves: intelligence gatherers/analysts and covert operators. On the one side are those who think the agency should confine itself to classic spying—finding out what the other side is up to. On the other side are those who think the agency should have the power to take action, to get involved and change the course of events, even if that means interfering with the affairs of other nations.

The split between these two differing views can be traced to some degree to the British secret service of World War II. At that time the British had a Special Operations Executive (SOE) for covert work and a Secret Intelligence Service (SIS) for intelligence gathering. There was an intense and bitter rivalry between the two groups. Donovan saw this disruptive rivalry during the war and set out to avoid it. In *The Second Oldest Profession* by Phillip Knightley, William Cavendish-Bentinek, former chairman of the British Joint Intelligence Committee, is quoted remembering something he said to Donovan about this:

> "Don't have two organizations; one for skullduggery, tripping people up, cutting throats, and any other nasty business like our SOE; another like our SIS for intelligence. Because they'd be quarrelling the whole time and trying to get the better of one another instead of getting the better of the enemy. Have one control organization." I didn't know I was acting as a midwife for that monster, the CIA.

According to the language of the 1947 National Security Act, it would appear that the CIA was being set up, as the CIG before it, solely as a sort of intelligence processing plant. The act lays out its duties, which include: advising the National Security Council on the intelligence activities of other government departments and agencies, bringing together and evaluating the intelligence that these other departments and agencies bring in, and performing "such other functions and duties related to intelligence . . . as the National Security Council may from time to time direct."

"Such other functions?" This open-ended phrase was essentially the green light that gave the CIA, at the discretion of the NSC, the authority to conduct covert operations. The intelligence community in the United States would never be the same again.

When the CIG became the CIA in September 1947, Vandenberg stepped down as director. The CIA's first director was Admiral Roscoe Hillenkoetter. He wasn't in office long before the CIA was directed by the NSC to carry out its first covert action, authorized by the "such other functions" clause.

The Truman administration was worried about Italy. In the chaotic years immediately following the war, the communist party had grown in strength. It now seemed quite possible that the party could win upcoming national elections. The Truman administration wanted to make sure that didn't happen. So, it turned to the CIA.

There was at that time a branch of the CIA called the Office of Special Operations. That branch has undergone a couple of name changes over the years—it's now called the Directorate of Operations. Whatever name it is officially called, people within the agency have always called it "Clandestine Services," for it is the arm of the CIA that carries out covert operations. The OSO's director during the Italian elections was James Jesus Angleton, the man who would later become the agency's high priest of *counterespionage*—ferreting out double agents and enemy spies, the most intricate and secret part of spying. As the agency's chief of covert operations, he set up the Special Procedures Group (SPG) to take care of the Italian problem.

Before the SPG began working, they checked with the agency's lawyers about the legality of attempting to interfere with the outcome of elections in another nation. Counsel informed the SPG that these actions weren't legal. Just as they have done many times since, they ignored their lawyers and proceeded anyway.

The covert operation carried out in Italy didn't involve mining harbors or assassinating foes. It was a secret war fought with propaganda and money. The CIA churned out reams of disinformation designed to discredit the Italian communist party—posters, false newspaper stories, pamphlets and the like. They also funneled a staggering $75 million into the coffers of the anticommunist parties.

The communists lost the election. There is some question about how much credit the CIA can claim for this result. For one thing, the United States exerted a great deal of pressure that wasn't secret. There were letter-writing campaigns, money was solicited from private citizens to help support the anticommunists and Truman quite bluntly threatened to cut off aid to Italy if the communists won. As well, the Italian people were quite aware of what was going on in Eastern

Europe and heard horror stories about Soviet tyrant Josef
Stalin. It's quite possible that the communist party quickly
lost its allure all on its own.

Whatever the various causes of the communist defeat, the
CIA claimed it as a personal victory. Truman was delighted
with the results of covert action. This president, who had at
first been wary of America having any peacetime intelligence
agency whatsoever, was so delighted that he decided there
should be a permanent, full-time covert action group. The
NSC directive 10/2, dated June 18, 1948, created the Office of
Policy Coordination (OPC), which was to remain separate
from the CIA and to report directly to the NSC. The CIA
retained the Office of Special Operations under Angelton, but
all covert actions were to be handled by the OPC. This separa-
tion of the CIA and the OPC was really just a matter of
bureaucratic organization. In truth, the OPC, run by ex-OSS
man Frank Wisner, operated as if it were a part of the CIA;
indeed, it wouldn't be long before the OPC was brought
entirely into the CIA fold.

The founding of the OPC was the first mention of the idea
of "plausible denial." This idea has become almost a creed of
CIA officers over the years. Directive 10/2 instructed that
"activities had to be so carefully planned and carried out that
any U.S. government responsibility for them is not evident to
unauthorized persons and that if uncovered the U.S. Government can plausibly disclaim any responsibility for them." In
other words, an operation had to be set up so that if caught,
the people at the OPC could lie about their involvement with
a straight face and with a good chance that they would be
believed.

At this time roughly three years had passed since Truman
had broken up the OSS and scattered it to the winds. In that
time the ex-OSS men in Washington, those who had served
under Donovan, had managed to build a new intelligence
agency out of the ashes of their own. They had reclaimed their
claws—the authority to spy, and their fangs—the authority to
conduct covert operations. In 1949, with the passing of the
CIA Act, the agency's powers were further expanded and

solidified. The act made the agency exempt from federal disclosure laws—it didn't have to report the "functions, names, official titles, salaries or numbers of personnel employed by the agency." In particular, DCI was given huge powers, including the authority to "spend money without regard to the provision of law and regulations relating to the expenditure of government funds."

Two things were readily apparent about the CIA in those early years. First, the founders of the agency had seen to it that American intelligence operations would be conducted under a very thick cloak of secrecy. Not only would the "other side" not know what the agency was up to, but the American public, even most elected officials, would be kept in the dark as well. This gave the agency the power to operate as the president and the NSC saw fit, free of the constraints that restricted the actions of other government agencies.

The second thing that was readily apparent about the CIA, even in these first years, was that covert operations took center stage. The split between the intelligence gatherers and the covert operators was there from the beginning, and it was deep. Apparently, the intelligence gathering—which to the world was all that the CIA did or was supposed to do—was going to have to take second billing within the agency. The ex-OSS men weren't content to simply *spy*, they wanted to *do* things, and when they looked around the world they saw several things that to their minds desperately needed doing.

4

GETTING OUT IN THE WORLD:
THE EARLY OPERATIONS

Many of the ex-OSS men in the CIA had worked with resistance groups throughout Europe during World War II. This cooperative effort had been one of the best ways to harass and subvert Germany's grip on the nations it had conquered. The OSS would drop agents into France or Yugoslavia. The agents would hook up with the local resistance and provide it with training, weapons and other support. They would also manage the very difficult task of bringing a country's feuding groups together to fight as a unified front. This work had been effective and successful.

At the end of World War II, the Soviet Union staked a claim to the influence of several countries in Eastern Europe, including Hungary, Czechoslovakia, Romania, Bulgaria and Poland. This was something like a kid in a schoolyard choosing who will be on his or her softball team. But these Eastern bloc countries (as they came to be known) had little say in whose team they were to be on. When the Soviet Union began to assert control over these countries, many of these OSS vets in the CIA thought that it would be a good idea to connect with and support the resistance groups struggling against this new conquering power.

Ex-OSS officer Robert McDowell tried to convince the Joint Chiefs of Staff that Soviet leader Stalin's grip on the Eastern bloc countries was not so tight and iron-fisted as the Soviets would have everyone believe. He was convinced that the Soviets were still awash in postwar chaos and that it was the ideal time to support resistance groups and partisans. McDowell's theory was that if, in response, Stalin were to clamp down even harder, the resistance would grow even stronger. McDowell also suggested that the United States work with émigrés who had fled their countries at the time of the communist takeovers. He felt that one day they could be used to release the various countries from Soviet control. McDowell presented his case well. The Joint Chiefs of Staff were convinced.

On orders from the Joint Chiefs of Staff, the CIA dropped hundreds of agents behind the Iron Curtain. As history soon showed, McDowell had been horribly wrong in estimating the strength and breadth of resistance in the Eastern bloc countries. In his defense, he himself had been convinced by the émigré leaders who desperately wanted to believe there were active resistance movements in their homelands. There weren't. One of the first places where this lesson was learned, and learned harshly, was Albania.

ALBANIA

Before 1948, Albania languished in relative obscurity, out of the eyes of American observers. When Albania was thought of at all it was dismissed as a "backward state." People weren't even sure where it was—"somewhere in the Balkans" was about as much as many people knew. Only when it became involved in the Yugoslavia/Soviet Union split in 1948 did Albania receive much attention.

Albania is a small country about the size of Switzerland, bordered by Yugoslavia and Greece. Its coast lies less than 100 miles across the Adriatic Sea from Italy. Geographically it is characterized by harsh mountains in the east and boggy lowlands toward the sea. Culturally, Albania has long been isolated from the rest of the world. This is largely because the Albanian language is unique, unrelated to neighboring Slavic and Greek tongues; indeed, not linked to any Western tongue.

Before World War II Albania had been a monarchy, led by King Zog. During the war, as part of the resistance battle against the Nazis the Albanian communist leader Enver Hoxha forged ties with the leader of the Yugoslavian partisans, Josip Broz Tito. After the war Hoxha, under the tutelage of Tito, took control of Albania, and King Zog was forced into exile. Tito once said he felt like an "elder brother" to Hoxha, and in those first postwar years Yugoslavia helped Albania get back on its feet, training the country's work force and supplying materials and food.

Having fled to Cairo, King Zog set himself up as a leader-in-exile. He claimed there was a broad network of loyalists in

Enver Hoxha (left), communist leader of Albania who came to power after World War II. [Credit: Bettmann Newsphotos]

Albania and Hoxha's grip on the country was weak. In 1947, Great Britain's Secret Intelligence Service (SIS)—now known as MI6—began parachuting agents into Albania to make contact with the promised legions of loyalists. The agents couldn't find them. Albanian émigrés in Greece and Italy trained by the SIS were sent on raids into their homeland, also to no effect. Britain was ready to give up on its attempts to foster unrest in Albania.

In 1948, however, the situation appeared to change dramatically. In Yugoslavia Tito became outraged at Stalin's attempts to involve the Soviet Union in his nation's affairs. This had been Stalin's pattern—to completely ignore local communist resistance groups that had fought during the war in favor of setting up governments that he could easily control. Quite simply, Stalin viewed the resistance groups as a threat. Most groups bowed to his pressure, but Tito, a fiercely independent nationalist, wouldn't put up with Stalin's meddling. In response Stalin had Yugoslavia expelled from the Cominform, the organization of communist states.

If Enver Hoxha viewed Tito as his brother, his father was Josef Stalin, and that's where his greater loyalty lay. As Yugoslavia split from Russia, so Albania split from Yugoslavia. Hoxha expelled all the Yugoslavian teachers and technicians from Albania and had his pro-Yugoslavian foreign minister Koci Xoxe arrested. A strong political gesture, perhaps, but not a practical one, for without Yugoslavian support the country fell apart. A French minister, Guy Menant, described the conditions there as "miserable," writing that "war is the only thing they have to look forward to."

Britain, which had been ready to suspend its anti-communist efforts in Albania, saw things differently after the split. It now appeared that continued covert action was both more plausible and also necessary. Albania was terribly poor and vulnerable; it was beginning to export revolution by supporting communist rebels in Greece (Italy, just across the Adriatic, might be next). Above all, it was a place where the Soviets could turn a foothold into a stronghold. Britain decided it would be a good time to shake the Albanian government hard and see if it would fall.

On December 16, 1948, Britain's Russia Committee, which had been set up to fight the Cold War (as the non-military conflict between East and West had become known), decided that while it wanted to do something about Albania it wouldn't do so without American involvement. The committee lobbied Frank Wisner, the chief of the Office of Policy Coordination (the covert action arm of the National Security Council), and the State Department and achieved an agreement. The agreement stipulated, however, that there would be no open action—Americans would not be dropped in Albania—but that they would fund and train the émigrés and partisans and oversee the operations.

The first order of business in 1949 was to choose a staging site for the operations. A U.S. base in Libya was considered and then discarded in favor of a British base in Malta. Frank Wisner joked to a member of Britain's MI6 that "whenever we want to subvert any place we find that the British own an island within easy reach." What makes this remark truly notable is that the man Wisner was talking to was Kim Philby, a man who would later become one of the most notorious figures in the history of espionage.

The next problem was the question of whom the British and Americans would work with. There were four major groups of émigrés at that time and four leaders—Midhat Frasheri in Turkey, Abas Ermenji in Greece, Said Kryeziu in Italy and King Zog in Egypt. They did not want to work together. Many things divided them. A major one was religion—the northern people were predominantly Roman Catholic, the southern were Moslem. Long-held, deeply ingrained family feuds and different basic politics (Abas Ermenji's group was fiercely antiroyalist and yet King Zog demanded that he be involved) added to the problem. In July 1949 a compromise was reached. A Zog nominee, Abas Kupi, was to chair a junta—a military government—with Ermenji and Said Kryeziu as deputies. Midhat Frasheri was put at the head of the Albanian National Committee, set up to promote their cause around the world.

The émigrés were trained in Malta by the British. The first group to be sent on a mission to Albania set out by boat in

September 1949. Not long after their boat landed, the party was met by security forces. In the ensuing gun battle three of the émigrés were killed; the rest managed to escape.

This was not a good sign, and the CIA began to lose interest in the Albanian operation. Some thought Hoxha was stronger than he seemed and that the chance of success was slim; others felt that with the Soviets now possessing nuclear weapons they should avoid direct conflict with the Eastern bloc. In 1950, however, Senator Joe McCarthy kindled the fires of rabid anticommunism, which swept across America. The CIA wasn't above the pressure to be staunchly anti-communist, and so the OPC was sent out to step up its anti-communist work in Albania. A second infiltration team set out from Malta, this time heading into Albania overland through Greece. By all accounts the mission was a bad joke. The Greeks hadn't been told of the mission and were naturally very suspicious of a bunch of Albanians trooping across their land—Albania was, after all, supporting the communist rebels in Greece. The Greeks had them all arrested. The Albanians were eventually released. They lay low for a time before attempting to enter Albania again. This time they were successful, but they found that once inside Albania they were hamstrung and immobilized—Hoxha's internal security was just too tight.

The joint U.S.-U.K. Albanian operation did not end, however. After another botched overland attempt, the émigrés parachuted in at night. They were all quickly captured. Sixteen men were dropped in a subsequent night flight, and their luck was no better. Those not shot on the spot were put on trial in the capital, Tirana, and those not given death sentences died anyway at the hands of the secret police.

Spirits sank on Malta and the rivalries and disagreements between the various groups of émigrés surfaced again. It was too much for the British and they pulled out. Not the CIA, though. The CIA was pinning its hopes on the skills of one émigré, Hamit Matjani. He had infiltrated Albania and had been able to move around and contact what resistance there was before slipping back out. In 1952, a team led by Matjani headed out from the Greek island of Kalanissia. Once inside

Albania they radioed back—Success! Over the next 18 months, through to the end of 1953, small groups—many of them Zog's royal guardsmen—followed Matjani into Albania and joined the underground. Finally, after almost six years of trying, the Albanian operation was on track. Or so it seemed.

On New Year's Eve 1953 a radio broadcast out of Albania gave the CIA a very rude shock. Tirana announced that Matjani had been in captivity essentially from the moment he had arrived a year and a half before. The Albanians had been manipulating the CIA into sending more men in after Matjani. All the men that had been sent during those 18 months had been shot or were about to be. Further, hundreds of their relatives had been killed in retaliation.

Why did things go so horribly wrong? When fingers are pointed over the Albanian fiasco, the first person they point at is Kim Philby, the British intelligence traitor who fled to Moscow in the 1960s. In 1949 no one suspected that this bright, witty, charming, well-educated "gentleman" could possibly be a double agent—at least almost no one. General Walter Bedell Smith, appointed as the new director of central intelligence in 1950, was highly suspicious of Philby. Smith swore he'd cut off intelligence relations with Britain unless Philby was removed as British intelligence representative in Washington. Philby was withdrawn from Washington, but that occurred some time after the Albanian operation had gotten off the ground.

Philby may well have betrayed the operation—after all, he was joint commander of the operation for a time. He, however, has denied it, and many believe him, speculating that he wouldn't have risked his position to thwart something as ultimately minor as that operation was. As well, some believe Philby's denial simply because he had gladly admitted—indeed gloated over—his other betrayals. On the other hand, he probably wouldn't want to take responsibility for the massacre of hundreds that occurred.

It seems likely that Philby informed his Moscow operators of the general plan of the Albanian operation, but it is doubtful that he betrayed individual missions. The real blame for the failure lies with U.S. and British intelligence for continuing to send the émigrés on missions when it was obviously a losing battle. Some credit this persistence to being blinded by their wishes—they wanted to beat the communists so much they only heard what they wanted to hear. Cynics think they weren't committed to winning at all: The Albanian operation was supposed to demonstrate to the Soviets that no matter how bad the odds, no matter how hopeless the fight, the CIA and SIS would stick it through.

Perhaps the most disturbing part of the Albanian operation was that it was not an isolated instance. In the early 1950s a group of CIA-trained and -funded Polish émigrés sneaked back into their country, set up a resistance network and radioed back for more men and gold. After a couple of years, as had happened in Albania, it was discovered to be a complete sham—the Poles managed to draw émigré anticommunist agitators home *and* milk the CIA out of millions of dollars in gold, all at the same time. The lesson finally learned from the attempts to foster antigovernment forces in Albania, Poland and other Eastern bloc countries was that the widespread resistance the CIA had hoped for simply wasn't there. The people were not happy with communism—far from it—but they were tired. They had been through a long and brutal war and had had enough. As well, the communists, with their ever efficient internal security services, made any resistance almost impossible.

The ultimate irony of the Albanian fiasco, of course, is that Albania didn't end up in the Soviet camp after all. When the Soviets under Nikita Khrushchev began their de-Stalinization in the 1950s, Hoxha, remaining loyal to the memory of Stalin, broke off relations between his country and Russia. He ended up in the camp of the Chinese, who had also split with the Soviets. Indeed, rather than becoming a Soviet pawn, Albania actually became something of a nuisance to the Soviet Union for decades.

HEAD TO HEAD WITH THE SOVIET UNION

The goal of the operations in Albania and Poland, and other equally unsuccessful missions in Lithuania and the Ukraine, was to "roll back the Iron Curtain." The CIA found, however, that it was next to impossible to get anything going in those countries. Worse, when it came to the ultimate target of these actions, the Soviet Union, there was no chance of success whatsoever—Russia, with its extraordinarily efficient and powerful security service, the KGB, was utterly impenetrable. Over the years, this hasn't changed. There is still essentially no way to get an agent into the Soviet Union. What the CIA hopes for are defectors—high-level officials who walk away and tell the West what they know. Best of all, they can occasionally recruit someone to become an *agent-in-place*—someone who remains in their position in Russia, passing out secrets. Every now and then they get a present out of the blue, a *walk-in*—someone who comes to them and offers to work as an agent-in-place. The CIA's fear with any and all of these agents, whether they're recruited or walk in on their own, is that they could be plants, or *double agents*.

When the United States dropped its first atom bombs on Hiroshima and Nagasaki, in August 1945, the bombs did more than just bring on a Japanese surrender and the end of the war; they changed the world, for their awesome destructive power meant that any future world war could bring about the destruction of all life on the planet. For several years the United States was the only country with nuclear weapons. They knew the Soviets would develop them. The question was when.

The trouble the CIA had in penetrating the Soviet Union became painfully obvious on August 29, 1949. On that day the Soviet Union detonated its first atomic bomb years ahead of predictions, taking the CIA completely by surprise.

Of course the whole reason for the CIA's existence was to eliminate such surprises. The agency was roasted over the coals for this intelligence failure. Director Hillenkoetter was ousted and General Walter Bedell Smith brought in.

An interesting thing about the spy business is that an intelligence failure can be worked to as great an advantage as a success. Just point a finger at the opposition's spy agency and say that they're more successful because they're bigger and more powerful. By the end of 1952, DCI Smith had expanded the CIA to 10,000 employees. He also gave the agency the basic organization that it has kept to this day. Smith created the Directorate of Plans—candidly called "Clandestine Services" within the agency—which officially brought covert operations fully under the CIA's control. This merged the NSC's Office of Policy Coordination and the CIA's old Office of Special Operations. The first director of Clandestine Services was Allen Dulles. Frank Wisner became his deputy and Richard Helms was chief of operations. All three of course were veterans of the OSS.

Because of the expansion and restructuring, the CIA was bigger and stronger than it had been before the Soviets caught everyone by surprise with their atomic bomb. One question still remained to be answered, however: How did the Soviets build their bomb so fast? The answer was obvious to many: They had stolen secrets.

While the CIA finds spying in Russia to be virtually impossible, the Soviets find no such trouble in America. The United States is an open society. There's no restriction of movement, no internal security service comparable to the KGB (the FBI works hard to ferret out spies, but it is not nearly as large or powerful as the KGB).

The KGB penetrated the American atomic energy program quite successfully. When Igor Gouzenko, attached to the Soviet embassy in Ottawa, defected, he unveiled a whole ring of Soviet spies operating in the United States and Canada. A married couple in the United States, Julius and Ethel Rosenberg, were arrested as spies and later executed for betraying atom bomb secrets. There was and continues to be some controversy over the case. Although supporters of the Rosenbergs have maintained their innocence over the years, it seems likely that they were indeed passing secrets to the Soviets. The question is, how much did it matter.

It's not as though the Soviets simply stole a bomb and set it off—they had been working in the field of atomic power since before the war. Indeed, some theorize that if their atomic program hadn't been cut off by the German invasion, they might have had the first chain reaction, before Enrico Fermi's in Chicago in 1942. Undoubtedly, they were behind the United States after the war, and they recruited as many German scientists as they could. The Soviet program only became urgent, however, after the bombing of Hiroshima and Nagasaki in the summer of 1945.

While the Soviets were on the course of building their own bomb anyway, they were nevertheless given a boost by spying. Their best informer was not the Rosenbergs but Klaus Fuchs, a German refugee who worked on British and American atomic projects, including Los Alamos, where the first bombs were built. He was discovered by the CIA in late 1949 and arrested and interrogated in England by MI5 (their internal security agency) in February 1950. Fuchs confessed to passing on incredibly damaging material on bomb design and theory and the state of American atomic research. It has been estimated that his betrayal saved the Soviets from a year to 18 months.

Walter Bedell Smith had replaced Hillenkoetter as DCI because of the CIA's failure to predict when the Soviets would become a nuclear power. Smith himself only lasted a few years as DCI, though not because the CIA was responsible for any great intelligence failure—in fact, he was promoted. In 1953, shortly after his inauguration, President Dwight D. Eisenhower asked Smith to join his White House staff and Smith accepted. Allen Dulles, then Clandestine Services director, was in turn promoted to the position of DCI. That made two members of the Dulles family in the Eisenhower administration, for Allen's brother, John Foster Dulles, was the secretary of state.

Allen Dulles had the perfect background for a DCI. A member of OSS in World War II, he worked out of Berne, Switzerland, running spies into Germany. His greatest coup was tapping into the ring of disillusioned officials in Berlin who wanted to assassinate Hitler (the war ended and Hitler killed himself before they got their chance). But his espionage experience went back even further, to spy work in Geneva during World War I. Dulles would often tell a classic story of missed opportunity that occurred in Geneva. One afternoon a Russian man he'd never heard of called to see him. Dulles took a look at the man in his waiting room and slipped out to keep a tennis date. The unnamed Russian man turned out to be Vladimir Ilyich Lenin, the soon-to-be leader of the Russian Revolution.

Dulles was generally regarded as perhaps the greatest spymaster in the history of U.S. intelligence. However, he was not a great administrator. He was terribly disorganized and shrugged off the DCI's role as coordinator of the intelligence community. Many found his sloppiness frustrating but were willing to put up with it. Eisenhower was quoted as saying, "I'm not going to be able to change Allen. I have two alternatives, either to get rid of him and appoint someone who will assert more authority, or to keep him with his limitations. I'd rather have Allen as my chief intelligence officer with his limitations than anyone else I know."

The years under Allen Dulles are often referred to as the halcyon days of the CIA, mostly because the agency, for the first time since manipulating the Italian elections, began to achieve some measure of success in the arena Dulles loved the most—covert action. Dulles didn't do all he wanted to—the Dulles brothers pledged to "roll back communism"—but under him the CIA did accomplish more than it had been able to before. One reason was precisely that the agency backed off from direct attempts to roll back the Iron Curtain. There were to be no more covert operations to stir up resistance. Instead, the CIA funded Radio Free Europe and Radio Liberty to broadcast America's message into communist lands. Instead of arming émigrés, they spent money freely, supporting noncommunist labor unions and youth movements throughout Europe and setting up research and policy-study institutes at home and abroad.

Most important though, the reason for the CIA's success during the Dulles years was that when it came to covert action, the agency turned its attention away from the Soviet bloc, where it found it had no chance of success, and focused its attention on countries it could penetrate—places where it could make a difference.

IRAN

One of the first targets of the CIA under Dulles was Iran. From 1951 Prime Minister Mohammed Mossadegh was in control of the country, with Shah Mohammed Reza Pahlavi serving merely as a figurehead. In the eyes of the Eisenhower Administration, Mossadegh had two big strikes against him. First, he was supported, if not controlled by, the Iranian communist party. Second, he nationalized the Anglo-Iranian Oil Company—that is, took it over in the name of his country. This was a very popular move with his people, who felt that the British were sucking Iran dry. The move was not quite so popular in England.

Britain asked the United States for help in blockading Iran and received it. The blockade certainly made things uncomfortable for Mossadegh, but in British Prime Minister Winston Churchill's view it still wasn't enough. He wanted more pressure brought to bear on Mossadegh—in fact, Churchill wanted him out.

Truman, however, hadn't been prepared to go that next step and had refused U.S. assistance. That all changed when Eisenhower became president and John Foster Dulles became secretary of state—they were quite interested in seeing a change of leadership in Iran. The CIA was given the go-ahead to oust Mossadegh.

The Iran operation is legendary at the CIA; legendary both for its success and for its simplicity. Kermit "Kim" Roosevelt, a grandson of Theodore Roosevelt—and, of course, a graduate of an elite college and an OSS veteran—was put in charge. The plan was simple—with a small band of operators and a suitcase filled with $2 million, Roosevelt was supposed to change the government of Iran.

Roosevelt and his team set themselves up in Teheran, working outside of embassy protection. When they needed help they would turn to the local CIA agents and a few members of

Iran's intelligence service. The goal was simple: Get Mossadegh out of office and replace him with Interior Minister General Fazollah Zahedi, who would then restore the power of the shah.

On August 14, 1953, confident of British and American support, the shah issued a decree declaring that Mossadegh was out of office and that Zahedi was the new prime minister. Perhaps the CIA thought things were going to go that simply, that smoothly, but they didn't. Mossadegh believed that the parliament and the people supported him, and so he countermanded the shah's decree, ruled that the shah's action was illegal, and seized complete control of the government.

The shah and his family panicked and fled to Baghdad, then on to Rome, where they were met by Allen Dulles. The shah was frightened—things were not going as planned. Dulles tried to allay the man's fears, telling the shah that everything would work out fine.

Back in Teheran, Roosevelt had to put his operation into high gear. The political situation in Iran was in turmoil, and Roosevelt knew that with a few deft moves things could turn and favor the United States. Using various forms of coddling and just plain bribery, he managed to bring a significant number of military and parliamentary leaders into his camp. He also mounted a propaganda campaign to win over the people; the showpiece was a huge anti-Mossadegh rally.

Mossadegh lost momentum and his support began to crumble. The forces opposed to him in the military went for the kill and staged a *coup* (a surprise takeover of a government). It was by no means a bloodless coup—many in the military had remained loyal to Mossadegh and fought hard to keep him in power—but was mercifully brief. In the end, just as the CIA had planned, Mossadegh was out and Zahedi was in. As expected, Zahedi soon invited the shah to return home. Upon his return, the shah took control and the monarchy was restored.

The following year, Western oil companies signed a 25-year lease agreement with Iran. As part of the agreement, the shah gave American interests 40 percent of Iran's oil. As Iran's oil flowed out, American arms flowed in. Military bases were set up, listening posts were built along the Soviet border and the CIA trained Iran's notoriously brutal secret police, the Savak.

In retrospect, of course, while the Iranian operation of 1953 was a resounding success at the time, the cost wasn't felt until 1979 when the shah was again forced to leave and the Ayatollah Khomeini seized power. Iranian resentment over American interference in their country's affairs had built from 1953 on. The result—Americans taken hostage at the U.S. embassy in Teheran and held for 444 days and Iran-sponsored terrorism against U.S. targets around the world.

Hindsight, of course, is 20/20, and there was no way then to predict what would happen in Iran 25 years down the road. Similarly, there was no way to predict what the consequences would be of another CIA operation of the mid-1950s, one that was conducted considerably closer to home, in Central America.

Ousted leader of Iran, Mohammed Mossadegh, being led into court. After the Shah assumed control of the country, Mossadegh was put on trial for high treason. [Credit: UPI/Bettmann Newsphotos]

GUATEMALA

Guatemala in the early 1950s was plagued with poverty and inequality. Two percent of the population owned 70 percent of the land. Of the desperately poor general population, half were illiterate. Moreover, the country was dominated by one corporation, the American-owned United Fruit Company. Guatemala was, at that time, a true "banana republic."

When Jacobo Arbenz Guzman was elected president of the country in 1951, he promised land reforms, trade unions and improved education. The United Fruit Company wasn't bothered by education programs, but the idea of land reforms and trade unions was very upsetting. And, like Mossadegh in Iran, Arbenz made the grave tactical error of tolerating and cooperating with his country's communists. Washington found this very upsetting.

In March 1953 a right-wing group, armed and financed by the CIA, attempted a revolution. It was a failure. But that didn't end the plan to oust Arbenz; in fact it almost spurred it on. Eisenhower wanted Arbenz out, and the CIA wasn't about to stop until it had satisfied its president.

With Allen Dulles's rise to the post of DCI, Frank Wisner became the deputy director of plans—the head of Clandestine Services. As the man in charge of covert actions, the Guatemala operation was his responsibility. Wisner chose Colonel Carlos Castillo Armas as a figurehead to lead the revolt. Wisner then set up bases in Nicaragua. Following the CIA's creed of "plausible denial," he arranged everything so that it would appear to be carried out by exiles and disaffected members of the Guatemalan military, not the CIA.

In addition to the military plans, Wisner started a propaganda campaign. A major part of the campaign was the Voice of Liberty, a radio station broadcasting into Guatemala from Honduras. The station was run by a man named David Phillips. Along with the basic, straightforward propaganda, Phillips injected judicious amounts of disinformation to undermine Arbenz—it worked. One piece of disinformation led Arbenz to suspect his air force of working for the CIA, which was untrue. Arbenz brought his suspicions to the commander of the air force, who was so enraged by Arbenz's accusation that he abandoned Arbenz—and, ironically, joined the CIA's side.

In the late spring of 1954, the army that Wisner had been building in Nicaragua was ready to roll. Before the invasion, Eisenhower stated: "I'm prepared to take any steps that are necessary to see that [this mission] succeeds. For if it succeeds, it's the people of Guatemala throwing off the yoke of communism. If it fails, the flag of the United States has failed." The one thing missing from the president's speech and from the words of other administration officials at the time is any mention of the fact that Arbenz had been democratically elected by the people of his country.

On June 18, 1954, Armas and the "Army of Liberation" crossed the border and entered Guatemala. They were supported in the air by P-47s flying out of Nicaragua, which bombed the vital Pacific port of San José. They were supported in the air in a different manner by David Phillips's Voice of Liberation radio broadcasts. Phillips made up reports of hard-fought battles and rebel victories that were accepted as fact—no one had any way to prove they were fiction—and this helped give Armas momentum.

Arbenz knew what was going on; he knew who was behind the revolt. In the United Nations, Guatemala's ambassador accused the United States of involvement. Because of the way Wisner had organized the operation, the United States was able to plausibly deny Guatemala's accusation, claiming that "the situation does not involve aggression, but is a revolt of Guatemalans against Guatemalans."

By June 27, Arbenz had had enough. He stepped down as president, handing the reins over to Colonel Carlos Diaz, the head of the Guatemalan armed forces. Much to the surprise and horror of the CIA, Diaz vowed to continue the battle and to crush the opposition. In response, the rebels sent in a couple of bombing runs on Guatemala City, and one hit the army's headquarters. The point was made. Diaz, who had been president for a day, was ousted and a junta took over. On July 2 the junta signed a pact with Armas, and he became president of Guatemala.

Armas then did as his backers asked of him: To eliminate the threat of another Arbenz being elected on the strength of his popularity among the poor, Armas disenfranchised much of the electorate by declaring that illiterate people couldn't vote. He also repealed the labor and union rights that Arbenz had granted. Armas took 800,000 acres that Arbenz had given to the peasants as part of land reform and gave them back to the United Fruit Company.

Many things have changed in the past three decades. The United States no longer uses Nicaragua as a place to train men to overthrow other countries. It uses other countries as a place to train men to overthrow Nicaragua. Nevertheless, as much as things change, they also stay the same. The population of Guatemala is still very poor and illiterate, and the vast majority of the people work land that is still owned by a tiny minority of the population.

The Iranian and Guatemalan operations were undeniable successes for the CIA. The agency was given tasks and they carried them out, without betraying U.S. involvement—at the time at least. They are, however, missions that are tainted by history, for both succeeded in placing in power regimes remembered for their brutality and supension of human rights.

In the remaining seven years of Allen Dulles's term as DCI (1954-1960), however, there were two operations that broke the mold at the CIA. One, the U-2 spy plane program, was the most fantastically successful and important operation in the history of espionage. The other, the attempted invasion of Cuba at the Bay of Pigs, was perhaps the worst embarrassment in the history of covert action. What makes the story of these two operations—the zenith and nadir—all the more fascinating is that they were both run by the same man.

5

RICHARD BISSELL: FROM THE U-2 TO THE BAY OF PIGS

There is a measure of stigma attached to mental breakdown in our society. If someone has appendicitis, we obviously don't hold it against that person. But if that person suffers a nervous collapse it's often viewed as a failure, as something he or she is responsible for and shouldn't have allowed. There's no such stigma in the CIA. To agency employees, given the inherent stresses of the work, it seems perfectly under- standable that someone could break. As ex-CIA officer Victor Marchetti and John Marks wrote in their book *The CIA and the Cult of Intelligence*:

> In the Clandestine Services, breakdowns are considered virtually normal work hazards, and employees are encouraged to return to work after they have completed treatment. Usually no stigma is attached to illness of this type; in fact, a number of senior officers suffered breakdowns while they were in the Clandestine Services and it clearly did not hurt their careers. Ex-Clandestine Services chief Frank Wisner had such an illness, and later returned to work as the CIA's station chief in London.

Frank Wisner's mental breakdown in 1957 didn't take everyone by surprise at the time. Years before, when Wisner was appointed the first head of the Office of Policy Coordination—the NSC's covert operations group, the first version of Clandestine Services—someone who had worked with him in the OSS was afraid the job would be too much for him, that it would kill him. Most people, though, thought Wisner would be perfect for the job. Although not a pure CIA blueblood—he came from the South, not the Northeast—Wisner did have most of the credentials. He was well educated and wealthy. (His CIA income was unimportant to him. His secretary once overheard him say he'd like a new car, so she put aside his CIA paychecks for a year, something he didn't notice, then handed the checks to him and said, "Mr. Wisner, here's your new car.") Most important, of course, he had been in the OSS. He shared a house in Wiesbaden, Germany, with Allen Dulles and Richard Helms at the end of the war and was the agent given the assignment of talking with Reinhard Gehlen, the German intelligence officer who had been spying on the Soviets. Wisner was viewed as a little pompous and self-satisfied at times by some, but all recognized that he was terribly smart and terribly hard working.

When Dulles became DCI, Wisner became the head of Clandestine Services, responsible for such successes as the Iranian and Guatemalan operations. But things were beginning to go seriously wrong for Wisner in 1956, when he left his desk in Washington for a whirlwind tour of CIA stations in Europe. His aides and the local CIA officials he met with noticed something amiss—Wisner had *too* much energy, *too* much enthusiasm; he was on some kind of manic high. Upon his return, that high began to fall apart. During a meeting Wisner interrupted everyone again and again with a rambling obscene story, and later he suffered a complete physical collapse. Wisner was hospitalized with a fever of 106 degrees. Apparently he was suffering from an undiagnosed case of hepatitis he had contracted eating raw clams in Greece.

One night in the hospital Wisner had an idea for a political cartoon and decided to call Philip Graham, publisher of the

Washington Post and a friend of his. His nurse, however, wouldn't give him a phone. "You don't know who I am," Wisner said to her, "but I have a very important job. And as part of my job I control thousands of *goons*. If you don't let me call Mr. Graham *I'm going to set my goons on you*."

Wisner returned to his job in the early part of 1957. Later, in the summer of that year, however, he suffered a breakdown at the CIA offices that couldn't be traced to bad clams. It was a full mental collapse, and Wisner had to be taken from the building by force and driven off in an ambulance. Wisner was gone from Clandestine Services for good.

When they write of Wisner's breakdown, Marchetti and Marks don't make it seem as serious as it was. On the advice of a colleague, Wisner entered a psychiatric hospital and underwent grueling rounds of electroshock therapy. He later said to that colleague, "If you knew what you'd done to me, you could never live with yourself." And although station chief in London is an important and respectable position, it was a long step down from chief of Clandestine Services. Wisner left the CIA for good in 1961, and in 1965, at the first sign of another mental breakdown, he took his own life.

The question in 1958 was who would replace Wisner as chief of Clandestine Services. During Wisner's assorted absences his deputy, Richard Helms, had filled in for him, and Helms seemed to be on track to take the position over permanently.

Helms was the quintessential *gray man* of intelligence: someone whose face one couldn't remember, someone who could disappear in a crowd of three. He lived in an unremarkable house, drove to work in an unremarkable car, and for all the world looked like a bureaucrat who toiled away at an unremarkable civil servant's job. His job, of course, actually was quite remarkable.

Helms wasn't part of the East Coast establishment that permeated the CIA. While well educated, he graduated from Williams, not an Ivy League school, and he didn't come from money. But he did have the most important credentials: He had been in the OSS.

Helms didn't start off to be a spy. In fact, his goal in life was to publish his own newspaper. With that in mind he took an absurdly low-paying job with UP's Berlin bureau in the mid-1930s. He traveled widely and wrote dispatch after dispatch, chronicling Hitler's consolidation of power and the growing threat of Nazism. By 1937, though, Helms had had his fill of world politics and returned to the United States. To further his ambition of owning a newspaper, he took a job on the advertising staff of the *Indianapolis Times.*

When America entered the war in December 1941, Helms received a commission in the Navy. He worked in New York City, plotting German submarine activity in the North Atlantic. During this time he was contacted by his old UP Berlin bureau chief, who was now with the OSS. Helms was invited to come aboard, but refused. He had a good job and the future of the OSS seemed uncertain. As fate would have it, though, in 1943 the Navy assigned Helms to the OSS.

He was given the basic spy training at a farm in Maryland—secret communications, sabotage, hand-to-hand combat and the like. But when his training was complete, Helms wasn't sent on daring missions to blow up oil depots and bridges. Instead, he was put into classical espionage—running spies. He ran his agents into Germany through secret intelligence operations in Scandinavia.

After the war, when the OSS was dismantled and eventually re-formed into the CIA, Helms successfully managed to make the transition. He did well in the CIA's early years and rose along with his fellow OSS veterans such as Wisner, Smith and Dulles. He had some contrary opinions about what a spy agency should do. For one thing, he was a staunch advocate of secret intelligence gathering as opposed to covert action. He was particularly displeased with the Guatemala operation, for although "successful," it risked exposing the agency. Yet he never let these opinions get in the way of doing his job. In others' eyes he was very smart, hardworking and well respected. Like any man heading up the ladder, he was also ambitious.

When Wisner left the post of chief of Clandestine Services, Helms wanted to be the one to replace him—after all, he had already shown he could do the job. Helms was almost certain to get the appointment. No one was more surprised than he when he didn't get it. And what made it worse was that the person who did get the job was Richard Bissell.

HELMS VERSUS BISSELL

Bissell was, in several ways, everything that Helms wasn't. Bissell was part of the Eastern upper class. He came from money and had the right education—he'd attended an exclusive boarding school and had graduated from Yale in 1932. What he lacked was the one major thing Helms had, and that was experience. Bissell hadn't been in the OSS. In fact, his expertise was not in espionage but in economics, which he taught at Yale and later at MIT before being drawn into the CIA in 1954 by some old friends.

But the rivalry between the two men was founded on more than just background; there was also a question of style. Bissell was tall, handsome and charming; Helms was nondescript and reserved. As Thomas Powers notes in his biography of Helms, *The Man Who Kept the Secrets*, Bissell's nickname was the more spirited, if juvenile, "Dickie," while Helms's was just plain "Dick."

But this difference in style went further than nicknames and who was more fun at parties; there was also a big difference in how the two men approached intelligence. Bissell was open-minded, willing to try anything, eager to kick out the jams and see what happened. While this led to some remarkable achievements—the spy plane and spy satellite programs in particular—it also tended to lead over cliff edges. Helms, on the other hand, considered things carefully. He wanted the agency to maintain a low profile and didn't much care for big and audacious operations. The irony in all of this, as we will see, is that despite their different ideas and approaches, both men ended their official intelligence careers under clouds of suspicion.

Helms may have resented Dulles for promoting Bissell over himself, but he nonetheless understood Dulles's reasons—Bissell's mind and his accomplishments. In the Helms biography, Thomas Powers writes this about Bissell's mind:

> It will not do to say simply that he was intelligent. The qualities which distinguished him were lucidity, a capacious memory, a tinkerer's love of system, and a confidence, unsettling in its coolness, that the only relevant question to be asked of a system was whether it worked.

And his accomplishments? Bissell didn't join the CIA until January 1954. That year he played a small but significant role in the Guatemalan operation and did a convincing study on the futility of mounting covert operations in the Soviet Union and its satellites. It was toward the end of the year that he began to make his mark, for from December 1954 on, Bissell was in charge of the most revolutionary operation in the history of intelligence gathering—the U-2 spy plane program.

THE U-2

The United States was worried. If American leaders had been stunned in 1949 when the Soviets detonated their first atomic bomb, years ahead of what the CIA had predicted, imagine how they felt in 1953 when the Russians set off their first hydrogen bomb—a far more powerful nuclear device—less than a year after America had exploded its first. Matters worsened in 1954 when, during the May Day military parade in Moscow, the Soviets unveiled a new swept-wing long-range bomber, the equivalent of the new American B-52. The frightening estimate was that by 1955 the Soviets would have twice as many of their new bombers as the United States would have B-52s. This was the so-called bomber gap—the first of many gaps to come.

There was an uneasy feeling in the U.S. military and intelligence communities that things were slowly getting out of control. It seemed as if the Soviet military were advancing by leaps and bounds, but there was no way to get any accurate information on what they were up to. It was essentially impossible to penetrate the Soviet Union with agents, and recruiting spies from within Russia took a long time. In addition to this, the spies who were recruited weren't always reliable.

Eisenhower's overriding concern was that there not be another Pearl Harbor, especially not a nuclear one. The United States and Canada had established the Distant Early Warning (DEW) line of radar stations across the Arctic. But with the new Soviet bomber, the DEW line could only give a two-hour warning, barely enough time to mobilize American nuclear forces. So, in 1954 Eisenhower set up the Suprise Attack Panel to study what could be done to eliminate the possibility of the Soviets successfully attacking without warning. The intelligence subcommittee of the panel stated outright that the United States should begin reconnaissance overflights of the Soviet Union as soon as possible. One trouble: No airplane had yet been built that would be able to fly such a mission.

In California, however, the president of Lockheed Aircraft, Clarence "Kelly" Johnson, was working on some ideas for just such a plane. Johnson was and is arguably America's preeminent designer of military aircraft. In 1943 he designed and produced the F-80, America's first jet fighter, in just 141 days. He was also responsible for the C-130 Hercules air transport (still a cargo workhorse) and the F-104 Starfighter. In 1954 Johnson had an idea for a plane that could fly for a long stretch and at an altitude of 70,000 feet.

The main problem of flying at 70,000 feet is that the air is so thin an airplane's engine has only 6 percent of the thrust it has at sea level. Therefore, you have either to carry more fuel, which increases the weight of the plane, or to design an incredibly fuel-efficient plane. Johnson chose the latter route and designed a strange hybrid craft, a cross between a glider and a jet, with the lightness and lift of the former and the speed—500 miles per hour or more—of the latter. Johnson took this design to the Air Force, but they turned it down, thinking it too fantastic. Johnson didn't give up, however. He managed to get his design before the intelligence subcommittee of the Surprise Attack Panel. They loved it and ran it by DCI Dulles, who was also impressed. Then, as the final step, Dulles and two members of the subcommittee took the idea to Eisenhower. The president was enthusiastic and gave his approval for the project on the spot. Dulles then summoned Richard Bissell to the White House.

Bissell had been excited about the project from the first moment he'd heard of it. Another bone of contention between Bissell and rival Richard Helms was the value each of them put on human intelligence, or HUMINT—the material they received from spies. To Helms, HUMINT was the bread and butter, the heart of intelligence. Bissell didn't trust it. To him, the proposed spy plane was ideal—a reliable, technical means of getting hard intelligence.

As Bissell later noted about that first meeting at the White House, it was all well and good to decide to build the plane. But no one had any idea how much it would cost, who would pay for it, where the plane would be built and tested, or who would fly it when it was built. Answering those questions became Bissell's job.

Bissell was originally assigned to handle only the CIA's part of the project. That part soon became the whole, both because of security concerns—the whole project had to be carried out in secrecy—and because Bissell wanted to run the entire show. In effect, he bought the CIA's way in by simply offering to pay for the whole operation, budgeted at $22 million, out of Dulles's contingency budget—money he could spend without having to get approval. Bissell ran the show as if it were a covert operation, with a small staff working in almost total seclusion.

In California, Kelly Johnson received the news of Eisenhower's go-ahead and went to work immediately. Within days he had assembled a crew of 23 engineers and had moved them into an empty hangar in Burbank. The project was given the name Aquatone and the plane itself was simply the Utility-2, or U-2. The engineers affectionately called it the "Angel," and in a joking reference to the absolute secrecy they were working under, they called the hangar "Skunk Works," after the clandestine distillery in the cartoon strip Li'l Abner. (The name stuck, and today, now that it is no longer top secret, Lockheed proudly points out Skunk Works in its promotional materials.)

The plane, however, was only one part, albeit the biggest, of the whole project. If the plane were to be used for spying, it would need equipment to do the spying. The Hycon Corporation of California built an enormous camera, the 450-pound B-camera, specifically for the project. A revolutionary lens was designed by Dr. James Baker, a Harvard astronomer, and a new Mylar-based film, the same thickness as Saran Wrap, was developed. The combination of this high-resolution film and lens produced a spy camera system that could pick out a tennis ball from an altitude of eight miles, and from the U-2's operational altitude of 13 miles, something the size of a newspaper page.

Once photographs were taken, they would need to be analyzed. Interpreting aerial photographs—photos taken from the air—is an exacting science. Photo interpreters learn to see things in aerial photographs that wouldn't be apparent to a casual observer. They learn how to recognize rail lines, hospitals, military installations, the model of each plane and tank, even missiles. To run the photo interpretation side of the project Bissell turned to America's foremost expert in the field, Art Lundahl. Lundahl was working at the University of Chicago when the CIA approached him. He accepted Bissell's offer. One reason he accepted is that he wanted to see photo interpretation get the attention it deserved in the intelligence community. Once called "the super salesman of photo inter- pretation," Lundahl was known for often quoting the Chinese proverb that a picture is worth 10,000 words, or, as he added, 1,000 spies.

Coordinating all of this was Bissell's job, and there were many who didn't think it could be done. The plane was the biggest problem. Air Force critics scoffed at the plans. If the plane even worked—which they weren't too sure about—it would take at least six years to build, and the project would certainly go way over the $22 million budget. Well, Johnson had the U-2 ready for its first flight on August 6, 1955, less than eight months after he was given the go-ahead, at a cost of $19 million, which was $3 million under budget.

With the plane built, the next question became who would fly it. First, in the fall of 1955, a team of Strategic Air Command officers was trained to fly the U-2. It in turn trained civilian pilots (in keeping with the CIA dictum of plausible denial, the whole project was to be passed off as civilian research, so the pilots could not be military officers). The pilots who signed on to the program probably did so both for patriotism and for the thrill of flying a plane that had hardly been flown before. There was the added incentive of a $30,000 annual salary, equivalent to what a senior airline official was earning at that time, and over $100,000 in today's dollars.

The pilots were trained in a desolate area of southern Nevada near the atomic testing grounds, an area Bissell had picked precisely so that it could come under the security protection of the Atomic Energy Commission. The training site, consisting of dry salt lake beds, was officially called the Watertown Strip and was known to the pilots as the "Ranch." One of the pilots, Francis Gary Powers, later remarked that it was a "you can't get there from here" kind of place.

The pilots soon learned that the odd, rather ungainly looking plane was not going to be easy to fly. With its 80-foot wingspan it must have seemed to be all wing and must have looked fragile and delicate; indeed, there was a rumor that each plane would be used only once. Indeed, the plane was incredibly light—made of advanced alloys with the best weight-to-strength ratio, and stripped down to the barest essentials. The plane would be flying 60,000 to 70,000 feet and yet the cockpit would not be pressurized. This meant that the pilots had to wear full pressure suits, like those worn by astronauts. The pilots had to be in their suits hours before the flights, getting accustomed to breathing pressurized oxygen.

The actual flying began with the trial of takeoff. The U-2's wings were so long and droopy that they were supported at each end by sticks, called pogos, on wheels. Crewmen would sit on the ends of the wings while the plane rolled down the runway. When the plane had gained enough speed to lift the wings, the crewmen would release the pogos and jump clear.

Once in the air, the U-2 held more surprises. For one thing, the long slender wings tended to flap noticeably, which didn't affect its performance but was undoubtedly disconcerting. At high altitude the plane's single jet engine was prone to flameouts. Luckily, this wasn't much of a problem because the pilot could simply glide down to a lower altitude and restart. Indeed, on some spy flights the pilot would shut the engine down on purpose, using the plane's gliding ability to conserve fuel. Whatever problems pilots had with the U-2 in the air, the biggest problem they faced in every flight was the prospect of landing the thing.

The first problem was getting it down onto the runway. With its 80-foot wingspan, the U-2 created so much ground effect—a build-up of pressure between the wing and the ground, which creates extra lift—that it would not land. The pilots had to get the plane to within a foot of the tarmac and then stall intentionally to get the craft to drop those last 12 inches. Then there was the problem of the landing gear: It was in bicycle formation, two wheels in a row, like a real glider. This meant that the plane would tip over onto one wing or the other when it slowed down. The pilots used to wager with one another about who could keep the plane steady enough during landing so that crewmen could stick pogos under the wingtips before the plane tipped over.

Despite the various trials and tribulations of flying the U-2, the pilots generally enjoyed it. As Gary Powers wrote in *Operation Overflight*, "There was only one thing wrong with flying higher than any other man had ever flown—you couldn't brag about it."

At the Geneva Summit Conference in July 1955, Eisenhower had suggested a rather interesting idea. Calling it the *Open Skies* proposal, he suggested that the United States and the USSR exchange blueprints of their respective military installations and allow each other to inspect these installations from the air. Soviet leader Khrushchev scoffed at the idea, calling it "nothing more than a bald espionage plot." Within a year, the United States had the ability to spy on the Soviet Union and there was nothing the Soviets could do to stop them.

A current model of the U-2 spy plane in flight. The U-2 was designed and built by Lockheed, which also built the U-2's successor, the higher and faster flying SR-71. Rumor has it that Lockheed is now building a spy plane that will fly above 100,000 feet and will be undetectable by radar. [Credit: Courtesy of Lockheed Aeronautical Systems Company]

Satisfied with the U-2 tests during that August, Bissell ordered another 22 of the planes at a price of $350,000 each. Early in 1956, a team of eight pilots, including Powers, was stationed at the Incirlik Air Force Base in Turkey. The first few operational flights of the U-2 merely skirted the borders of the Soviet Union, intercepting radio and radar signals. In early June 1956, DCI Dulles and Bissell went to Eisenhower with the news that the U-2 was ready for its true mission—to cross the border and fly right over the Soviet Union. Eisenhower gave his go-ahead the next day; they had a 10-day period to spy on Russia.

The first four days passed with the Soviet Union hidden under cloud cover. On the fifth day, July 4, 1956, the skies opened and the U-2 took off on its first overflight of the Soviet Union. Dulles checked with Bissell to see if the plane had gotten off the ground. According to Thomas Powers' *The Man Who Kept the Secrets*, Bissell replied, "Yes, sir, it's in the air now." When told that the flight plan took it over Moscow and Leningrad, Dulles gasped, "My God. Do you think that's wise, for the first time?" Bissell replied that it would be easier that first time than at any other time.

The flight was a success. Unfortunately, the most important intelligence the flight gathered was the discovery that Soviet radar was better than had been thought. Bissell had hoped that the plane would be able to make its flight undetected. No such luck. The plane was picked up on radar shortly after it violated Soviet airspace and was tracked throughout its flight. It set off more than radar alerts, though—the Soviets were furious, so furious, in fact, that Eisenhower put a hold on flights for a month. Much of the rage must have been out of frustration, for the plane couldn't be touched, flying above the operational ceiling of Soviet surface-to-air missiles (SAMs).

The U-2 essentially changed the world of superpower politics. The United States, once blind, could now see. In their various flights across the country, the planes either followed a looping pattern or went straight across the country from Turkey or Pakistan to Norway. The U-2s took pictures of every inch of the Soviet Union; from those photographs Art Lundahl and his photo interpreters noted every airfield, every military base, and every submarine pen the Russians had.

One immediate result: The bomber gap was closed. It was discovered that the Soviets didn't have squadron upon squadron of its new bomber. At military parades a seemingly endless number of the bombers would fly by. The U-2s found out that the Soviets had just a few of those bombers, but they would have them circle back and fly over the parade again, giving the illusion of having many, many more than they actually did.

But, all good things must come to an end.

Originally it was thought that the U-2 would have an operational life of only two years or so before the Soviets improved their SAMs to the point of reaching 70,000 feet and bringing down a U-2. As it happened, the U-2 was able to fly over the Soviet Union for four years, much longer than had been initially thought. And, as it turned out, a little longer than was safe.

In mid-April 1960 Bissell went to Eisenhower with a request for a flight. Eisenhower had maintained close control over the flights, even suggesting flight paths on occasion and approving them one by one. Secretary of State Christian Herter was present during Bissell's request and voiced his objection: With the Paris Summit Conference scheduled for May, Herter thought it would be a bad time for a U-2 to be shot down. Eisenhower said that no time would be a good time for a U-2 to be shot down and gave his okay.

The pilot selected for the flight was Francis Gary Powers. He was to fly from Peshawar, Pakistan, straight across the Soviet Union to Bodo, Norway. After many days' delay because of cloud cover over Russia, the skies finally cleared. The plane took off at 5:20 A.M. on May 1, 1960. It is perhaps ironic that the U-2's first flight over the Soviet Union took place on July 4, America's biggest holiday, and that the last flight took place on May 1, May Day, an important day of celebration for the Soviets and all communists around the world.

Powers was picked up by Soviet radar the moment he crossed the border. SAM sites along his projected flight path were alerted. For Powers it was an uneventful flight until, nearing the halfway point, he passed near Sverdlovsk. Suddenly, without warning, the plane was hit. "I can remember feeling, hearing and just sensing an explosion . . . everywhere I looked it was orange. I said, 'My God, I've had it now.'"

Powers barely managed to escape and parachute to safety while the plane crashed. There were two things, however, that he did not do that subjected him to harsh criticism. First, he failed to arm the self-destruct mechanism, which was supposed to destroy the plane and eliminate all evidence of spying. Powers claimed that the way the plane was falling pulled him out of the plane after he had been able to flip only one of the two switches needed to arm the self-destruct.

The second complaint some people had regarding Powers was that he had not killed himself. The pilots were given a fake

Downed U-2 pilot Gary Powers sits in the defendant's dock during his espionage trial in Moscow. Powers could have received the death penalty, but instead received a 10-year sentence. He was later exchanged in a spy swap with Soviet agent Colonel Rudolph Abel. [Credit: UPI/Bettmann Newsphotos]

silver coin with a poisoned needle concealed inside that they were to use if they wanted to take their own lives. Powers and the CIA have since maintained that suicide was presented only as an option and not as a requirement. Not everyone was happy. Eisenhower's son John cried, "The CIA promised us that the Russians would never get a U-2 pilot alive. And then they gave the S.O.B. a parachute!"

The reason people wanted the plane destroyed and Powers dead was that that was the only way the CIA could achieve its goal of plausible denial. Initially, when it was assumed the plane had been destroyed and the pilot killed, the United States claimed that the U-2 was an atmospheric research plane on a scientific flight. But then the Soviets revealed they had both wreckage that was fairly intact and a live pilot. The United States was caught in a lie. The U-2 incident was a propaganda windfall for Khrushchev. He used it as an excuse to storm haughtily out of the Paris Summit. Later, the wreckage of the U-2 was put on public display in Moscow, and Powers was tried on television. Things eventually calmed down and in the end Powers was exchanged in a spy swap for Colonel Rudolph Abel, a Soviet agent caught in New York. Powers returned to the United States and managed to live in relative obscurity, eventually taking a job as a helicopter pilot for a Los Angeles television station. He died in 1977 when his helicopter crashed.

To many in the U.S. government though, the worst part of the U-2 incident was not the propaganda defeat—it was the loss of the U-2 as a source of intelligence. Never again would an American spy plane overfly the Soviet Union. In the long run it didn't matter. This was because the whole time he was working on the U-2, Bissell was also overseeing a far more ambitious program of technical spying—satellite reconnaissance. Within a year of the U-2's downing, Art Lundahl and his team of interpreters were poring over photographs of Russia taken from space.

The U-2 program had been a resounding success, and Bissell deserved much of the credit. Kelly Johnson and his Skunk Works crew built the plane; others built the camera; and Art Lundahl interpreted the pictures. But it was Bissell who brought it all together.

Bissell had been impressive, and there was no one he impressed more than his boss, DCI Allen Dulles. It was primarily on the strength of Bissell's U-2 work that Dulles promoted him to deputy director of plans—chief of Clandestine Services—after Wisner's mental breakdown.

But building a spy plane and running America's covert operations are somewhat different tasks. Whereas Bissell's unbridled enthusiasm and "Let's do it!" mentality was what was needed to get the U-2 off the ground, it was also a characteristic that could get him and a nation into trouble. If Bissell once thought anything was possible, his U-2 success made him believe it. But not just anything *was* possible, especially not a secret invasion of Cuba.

THE BAY OF PIGS

Pundits have it that if Fidel Castro had been a better baseball player there would still be casinos in Havana. Indeed, before he became a revolutionary and the leader of a communist country, Castro had ambitions to play in the majors. The man

Fidel Castro, leader of Cuba, is shown here in 1959, not long after his revolutionary forces took control of the country. [Credit: UPI/Bettmann Newsphotos]

who would one day decry Yankee aggression once had a tryout with the New York Yankees.

In November 1956 Castro began a somewhat different career. After some time abroad, he returned to his native Cuba with a mere 81 followers. His goal was nothing less than to overthrow the dictatorship of the conspicuously corrupt Fulgencio Batista. No one gave Castro much chance of success, but on New Year's Eve, 1959, he surprised everyone by entering Havana and taking control of the Cuban government.

There has been some disagreement over the years as to whether Castro was simply a *nationalist* (someone who wanted to end the foreign control of his country) who later turned communist or a communist right from the start. This is discussed in light of the U.S. reaction to Castro's revolution, which was not at all friendly. The question is did Castro turn to the Soviets because he couldn't get the help and support from America that he needed, or was he planning on cutting a deal with Moscow from day one. The answer now appears to be somewhere in the middle. While Castro's thinking was Marxist from an early stage, he probably didn't plan on the Soviets becoming quite so involved in his country as they have since become.

At any rate, the United States grew very alarmed when Castro seized American assets in Cuba, vowed to support rebels against any U.S.-backed dictatorship in Latin America (a popular sentiment in the region after the United States aided in the overthrow of the government in Guatemala) and established friendly relations with the USSR.

The head of the CIA's Western Hemisphere Division wrote to Allen Dulles, stating the obvious: The United States now had a communist country 90 miles from Miami. He suggested that "thorough consideration be given to the elimination of Fidel Castro—the disappearance of Fidel would greatly accelerate the fall of the present government."

Dulles concurred. He took the matter up with the NSC. The NSC in turn created a Special Group to look into the various possible actions that could be taken against Castro. The Special Group then put the matter back in the hands of a

CIA task force, which was to carry out the group's wishes. The wish list included creating a force of armed Cuban exiles for an invasion, establishing a network of subversives within Cuba, and, if possible, assassinating Castro, his brother Raul and fellow traveler Ché Guevara.

As deputy director of plans, Bissell considered this his ball game, and he took to it with vigor. Over the ensuing years, the CIA concocted, and on occasion even tried, some rather bizarre schemes to get rid of Castro. Some of them weren't even designed to kill him, the theory being that a dis-empowered Castro would be better than a martyred one.

In one plan, CIA agents were going to spray a television studio where Castro was going to give a speech with LSD powder, so that in the middle of the speech he would start act-ing as if he had lost his mind. In another plan agents were going to wait until Castro stayed in a hotel and left his shoes outside his door to be polished. They would then sprinkle the shoes with thalium salts. The salts would then enter Castro's bloodstream through his feet and cause his hair to fall out. The theory was that, like Samson shorn of his locks, in a country where a leader's macho image was crucial, a Castro without his characteristic beard would lose the support of his people.

Other plans were less goofy and more straightforward. These were plans to kill him. The task force considered giving him a gift of poisoned cigars. They more seriously pursued a plan to taint Castro's food with botulin, a deadly poison. They went so far as arranging with an unfaithful member of Castro's staff to do the poisoning, but when the man was fired the plan fell through.

Assassination plots make strange bedfellows, and perhaps the most disturbing plan involved asking the Mafia to kill Castro. The CIA used former FBI man Robert Maheu to con-tact Las Vegas–based mob boss John Rosselli. Rosselli in turn brought in the notorious Mafia boss Sam Giancana and Santos Trafficante, the head of the Cuban mob. Ultimately the plan fizzled out, but not before the FBI got wind of it. They were not pleased by the idea of the CIA working with people they were trying to prosecute. The CIA, however, had no problem with the plan. The agency has often firmly believed in the utilitarian maxim that the end justifies the means.

Meanwhile, plans to invade Cuba with a Cuban exile force proceeded apace. The original plan had been small. The idea was to train 25 Cuban exiles in Panama; they would in turn train a small, elite corps. This crack unit would then secretly invade Cuba, connect with the network of anticommunist resistance, and bring Castro down. Ironically, the plan seemed to mimic the way Castro himself had seized power, working initially with only a small group.

Unfortunately, the plan also resembled the plans to bring down the communist governments of Albania and Poland a decade before in that it involved using exiles to connect with a resistance inside the country. As in Albania and Poland, it was discovered that such a resistance really didn't exist; an invasion force wouldn't be carried into Havana on the shoulders of a public uprising.

Instead of canceling the invasion plans, however, Bissell simply changed them and made them bigger. Eisenhower approved $13 million for the operation, and by the time John F. Kennedy was elected president in November 1960, a relatively large-scale invasion plan was in full gear. An invasion force of 1,300 Cuban exiles had been put together. For air support, exiled Cuban pilots were being trained on B-26 bombers by Alabama National Guardsmen. David Phillips, who had run the propaganda show during the Guatemalan operation, was back, operating a Voice of Liberty-type radio transmitter from Swan Island off the coast of Honduras. For Bissell, everything was going relatively smoothly with the preparations except for one nagging problem—Richard Helms.

Helms was not a big fan of the Cuban invasion plan. It wasn't on moral grounds that he differed with Bissell, for he had no problem with the idea of ousting Castro—if that's what the president wanted then Helms would try to see it through. The problem was, as Thomas Powers notes in his

Helms biography, that "Helms and Bissell differed very greatly on how to go about it."

> To begin with, they had differing standards of secrecy. When Helms said secret he meant *secret* . . . secret from inception to eternity. Bissell meant secret from the *New York Times*, at least until the operation was successfully completed.

To Helms, the Cuban invasion plan was a nightmare secrecy-wise. Although the troops were being assembled and trained in Honduras, the operation was being run from Florida under the cover of the University of Miami, using print shops, gun shops and coffee shops as further fronts. So far as Helms was concerned it was filled with holes, an easy operation for Cuban spies to infiltrate. And there was alarming evidence that it had been infiltrated. In fact, well before the invasion Castro began talking openly about U.S. plans for invasion. Helms felt it was absolutely necessary that James Angleton and his counterintelligence staff have a crack at sealing up the mess.

Bissell bristled at this interference; indeed he bristled somewhat at all of Helms's work in the operation. He accused Helms of foot-dragging, if not outright obstruction, and according to some sources, on two occasions went to Dulles and requested that Helms be reassigned, preferably to London. This would have essentially ended Helms's intelligence career, but luckily for him, the transfer never happened. As history would have it, it wasn't Helms's career that was terminated by the attempted invasion, but Bissell's.

In retrospect, there were many things that signaled doom for the operation. As the date for the invasion approached, Kennedy, not long in the Oval Office, began to waffle over this thing he had inherited from Eisenhower. In Kennedy's mind he was caught between a rock and a hard place. He didn't want to scrap the plan altogether because he didn't want to appear soft on communism. On the other hand, he didn't like the idea of such a big and splashy operation. He reached for a compromise. Air cover would be reduced. The landing

Cuban artillery shown firing on CIA-backed rebels during invasion at Bay of Pigs.
[Credit: UPI/Bettmann Newsphotos]

site for the operation would be switched to a beach that some believed would be easier to take with minimal naval and air support, a place called the Bay of Pigs.

Early in the morning of April 17, 1961, 1,300 CIA-trained Cuban exiles, escorted by U.S. vessels, invaded Cuba at the Bay of Pigs. It was a disaster from the start. What minimal air cover there was didn't last long. After the first aerial strike caused an instant international uproar, Kennedy canceled the second. One hundred of the Cuban exiles were killed in the fighting, and the remainder were rounded up by the afternoon. It was a major propaganda victory for Castro, dramatically increasing his popularity among the Cuban people.

Kennedy did the smart thing, perhaps the only thing a president could do: He accepted full responsibility for the catastrophe. To many in the CIA that seemed only right, for to them Kennedy was responsible for the failure. Even Bissell said, "this war *might* have been lost on the ground. It *was* lost in the air." In the flurry of finger-pointing, however, a number of fingers were pointed at Bissell as well.

For one thing there was the problem of the lax approach to secrecy, something that Helms had been aware of but which Bissell didn't spend much time thinking about. This became an issue when, only a few days before the invasion, Castro did a sweep of dissidents on the island. Up to 100,000 people were jailed, including all of those who might have been expected to pick up the rallying cry of the invasion.

But the biggest problem with Bissell's plan was simply a matter of numbers. An invading force of 1,300 recently trained exiles against a regular army of 200,000 does not make for very good odds. To be fair to the Bissell plan, the invasion wasn't supposed to bring about an immediate overthrow of Castro. The idea was to secure a position, and have the United States recognize the rebels and vow to defend them. From that point Bissell hoped they could bring in the United Nations and eventually force elections. In retrospect it seems a rather risky plan. Some have theorized that Bissell's hidden agenda was to get the ball rolling to such a degree that Kennedy couldn't stop it. Kennedy would have to break his no-military-intervention vow and send in the Marines. In the long run, whatever Bissell's plan was, secret or otherwise, it didn't work.

THE AFTERMATH

Although Kennedy took all the heat in public, in private he spread it around. He was furious with the CIA and at one point threatened to break it into a million pieces and scatter it to the winds. After he calmed down a bit, he settled for making some major personnel changes. The first to go would be DCI Allen Dulles. Kennedy reportedly told America's great spymaster: "Under a parliamentary system of government it is I who would be leaving office. But under our system it is you who must go." An irony of Dulles's departure was that he never got to occupy his office at the brand new, $47 million CIA headquarters, which he had built in Langley, Virginia, just outside of Washington.

CIA Director Allen Dulles (center), in a car with President John F. Kennedy (left). The "Golden Years" of the CIA with Dulles at the helm came to an end with the Bay of Pigs. Kennedy asked Dulles to resign in the wake of the disastrous Cuban invasion attempt in April 1961. [Credit: UPI/Bettmann Newsphotos]

Bissell survived a little longer, but not much. His neck was put on the chopping block when an internal CIA report on the operation was finished, laying much of the blame at his feet. He didn't go out immediately, however. The new DCI, John McCone, even got Kennedy's permission to have Bissell stay on as the head of a new directorate McCone wanted to set up, the Directorate of Science and Technology. Bissell considered the offer—the new directorate would be responsible for, among other things, Bissell's babies, the spy planes and spy satellites—but, in the end, turned it down.

The near-unanimous choice to succeed Bissell as chief of Clandestine Services was Richard Helms. Strangely, by the time Helms took over at Bissell's job, much of the rivalry and bitterness between them had faded. There was something about how everything had happened—the Bay of Pigs failure and Bissell's defeat—that seemed to change things between

the two men. In the Helms biography, Thomas Powers·tells
of a dinner given to honor Bissell upon his leaving the CIA in
February 1962:

> There were toasts after the meal, the sort of thing usual on such
> occasions, expressions of friendship and regard, but all the same
> Bissell was at first surprised and then touched—even moved would
> not be too strong a word—at the grace and warmth of Dick Helms's
> short speech. It was as if the tension between them had never been.

6

YEARS OF CHANGE: ASSASSINATION PLANS AND SECRET WARS

It might seem as if Richard Helms was a man of contradictions. Appointed after the fall of Richard Bissell to be the new chief of Clandestine Services, Helms was often opposed to many covert schemes. But Helms himself didn't see any conflict of interest. To him, what he thought about covert operations was really beside the point. Sure, he would suggest other courses of action and try to bring others around to his view, but he ultimately would do what his superiors asked of him, and he would give it his all. He viewed himself and the CIA as servants to the president and his designates. He would do as they asked. Richard Helms was a company man.

It's important to keep this in mind—that Helms separated his private opinions from his duty. Because when one simply looks at the course of subsequent events, it doesn't seem that there was much change when the new DCI, John McCone, took over from Dulles, and Helms took over from Bissell in 1962. Yes, McCone created a new directorate, the Directorate of Science and Technology, to run the agency's technical means of intelligence gathering, such as the satellites. But there were still plots to overthrow unfriendly governments and assassinate unfriendly leaders.

It is nevertheless ironic that years later, in the mid-1970s, during the Senate investigations into alleged CIA wrong-doings, it would be Helms who would take much of the heat for many of the more questionable covert operations that had occurred since the early 1960s. Some of these operations were run by Helms from the beginning, others—most notably the plots to assassinate Castro—he had inherited from Bissell. What's most ironic is that one operation Helms took a particular amount of heat for was run entirely by Bissell and was over before Helms became the deputy director of plans.

THE CONGO/ZAIRE

Before June 1960, the country we now know as Zaire, in Central Africa, was the Congo, a colonial holding of Belgium. In the 1950s and 1960s there were independence movements within most of the colonies in Africa; the Congo was no exception. There were several factions within the colony struggling for independence. Belgium didn't want to lose this holding, but the pressure became too much to bear. In June 1960, Belgium granted the nation independence. One might think that the forces that had struggled for in-dependence within the country would be elated. They weren't. They were excited to have independence, but the way in which Belgium granted it was destructive. Belgium made no preparations for anything like a smooth transition from colonial to home rule. Belgium simply pulled up its stakes and left.

The result was instant chaos. Patrice Lumumba had been elected as the new country's first prime minister, but he was having a hard time maintaining control. He had three quite considerable problems to handle. First, under the leadership of Moise Tshombe, the province of Katanga had seceded from the new nation. Second, much of the army supposedly under Lumumba's control was openly rebellious. Third, while Belgium had left abruptly, it still had a presence in the country; there were a good number of Belgian troops still loitering about.

Lumumba asked the United Nations for help, and the United Nations agreed, up to a point. A U.N. peacekeeping force was sent in to help stabilize things, but the United Nations drew the line at helping Lumumba bring the province of Katanga back into the country. Lumumba then did the one thing that has provoked the anger of the United States so often: He called the Soviets. The Soviets do not hesitate over such invitations. On August 26, 100 Soviet bloc technicians and 10 Soviet transport planes arrived in the capital of Leopoldville.

While the arrival of the Soviets seemed to be a turning point, the CIA had in fact been looking at ways of getting rid of Lumumba for some time. Lawrence Devlin, the CIA station chief in the Congo, had cabled home: "There may be a little time left in which to take action to avoid another Cuba." He received a cable in return: "You are authorized to proceed with operation."

Devlin didn't waste any time. He quickly set up relations with the anti-Lumumba factions within the country. The person who was to serve as the head of the anti-Lumumba forces was the country's president, Joseph Kasavubu. In the Congo, as it is in many countries with both a president and a prime minister, the president is more of a figurehead while the prime minister has the power. In Britain, the equivalent is the relationship between the Queen and the prime minister. The figureheads in these positions often do have quite formidable powers but, according to tradition, never use them. Kasavubu, as the figurehead of the Congo, broke with tradition and, on September 5, 1960, declared that Lumumba was no longer prime minister. In his place Kasavubu put a military leader, Colonel Joseph Mobutu.

Lumumba sought and received protection from the U.N. forces in the country. Even with Lumumba out of office, however, Devlin was not satisfied. He wanted Lumumba crushed—he was afraid Lumumba would reappear on the scene, either on his own strength, or through the workings of the Soviets.

Ousted Congo Premier Patrice Lumumba in custody in December 1960. Lumumba was a CIA assassination target. Before he could be killed by CIA operatives he escaped, only to be caught and killed by rival Congolese forces. [Credit: UPI/Bettmann Newsphotos]

To crush Lumumba meant to kill him. Bissell's assistant for scientific matters in Clandestine Services, Sidney Gottlieb, was brought in. Gottlieb, a PhD in biochemistry, was told to develop a poison that would mimic an African disease. The idea was to kill Lumumba in such a way that his death would seem natural—a way that wouldn't make him a martyr and wouldn't be traceable to the CIA. Gottlieb developed his poison and was sent to the Congo to oversee its use. It was soon discovered that there was no way to get it to Lumumba, and Gottlieb returned home.

There had been a back up plan, however, one that ignored the subtlety and sophistication of exotic poisoning: Lumumba would simply be shot. The CIA trained two men to make the hit. The assassins were code-named "WI/ROGUE" and "QJ/WIN."

Bissell asked CIA officer Justin O'Donnell to run the assassination plot, but O'Donnell was a strict Catholic and refused—he agreed to flush Lumumba out of U.N. custody, but he did not want to be directly involved in the murder. When Bissell continued to press him, O'Donnell protested to Helms. Helms supported him, saying he was "absolutely right" in refusing the assignment. The plan proceeded without O'Donnell and the services of QJ/WIN were requested for the actual assassination.

Before an assassination attempt could be made, however, Lumumba slipped out of U.N. custody in Leopoldville of his own free will. He headed for Stanleyville, from where he wanted to mount a countercoup against Mobutu. Mobutu's troops worked with the CIA network within the country to block roads and search for Lumumba. Lumumba was captured in this dragnet. The CIA's plan then was to have Lumumba sent to Bakwanga prison, a place so notorious for its horribly high death rate among prisoners that it was given the nickname the "Slaughterhouse."

Lumumba never made it to Bakwanga. The plane taking him there veered off course and landed in the rebel province of Katanga. On January 17, 1961, Patrice Lumumba was murdered.

There was never anything to connect Lumumba's actual murder to QJ/WIN, Devlin, O'Donnell or the CIA in general. By all accounts, he was killed by his fellow Congolese. Nevertheless, the CIA had been in the country and had tried to kill him. The Church Committee investigation into the CIA in the mid-1970s found that "the testimony is strong enough to permit a reasonable inference that the plot to assassinate Lumumba was authorized by President Eisenhower." In the mid-1970s, however, it wasn't Eisenhower who took the heat, nor Dulles, nor even Bissell. It was the man from that period who had most recently been the director of the agency—Richard Helms.

OPERATION MONGOOSE—THE CONTINUING WAR AGAINST CASTRO

As mentioned earlier, Richard Helms had problems with the Bay of Pigs operation. These were not on moral grounds, but because he didn't like covert operations that drew attention to the CIA. As Bissell's successor at Clandestine Services, he would continue to seek the removal of Castro, but he sought lower-keyed routes. The policy against Castro continued because of President Kennedy. Despite his apologies to the American people and the world for the Bay of Pigs, Kennedy, like Eisenhower before him, wanted Castro gone.

Perhaps it was *because* of the Bay of Pigs fiasco, and having to eat so much crow for it, that Kennedy became so obsessed with removing Castro from power. In the summer of 1961 the White House set up the Counter-Insurgency (CI) Group. The name falsely represented its function. The focus of the CI Group became Cuba, and its goal was to promote insurgency there, not counter it.

The code name given this second phase of the U.S. government's continuing war against Castro was *Operation Mongoose*. The man the CI Group put in charge of overseeing Mongoose was General Edward G. Lansdale, a man with near legendary experience in counterinsurgency in the Philippines and Vietnam. He was a man noted for coming up with rather "creative" solutions. In the Philippines, he drove communist insurgents out of an area by preying on a local superstitious fear of vampires. Lansdale's men abducted and killed a rebel, put two puncture holes in his neck, drained the blood from the body and threw the corpse back onto the trail. The rebels fled. In Vietnam, Lansdale was given partial credit for American-supported Ngo Dinh Diem's landslide election. One reason: Lansdale chose the colors for the ballots—Diem's name was printed in red, his opponent's in green. In Asia, red is the color of good luck; green is the color of the cuckold (one whose wife is unfaithful to him).

While Lansdale would be overseeing Operation Mongoose, the CIA would be doing the actual work. The man the agency chose to run the show was William Harvey, a rather legendary figure in the history of the CIA. He was legendary for his bulk, his drinking and his handguns: Harvey was so fat that he received a special dispensation from the CIA allowing him to fly first class at the agency's expense because his bottom was too big to fit into economy-class seats. Harvey described himself as a three-martini-lunch man—two doubles and a single. He brought a different handgun from his collection to the office every day and laid it on the desk. This last quirk wasn't always viewed with amusement. As Thomas Powers writes in his Helms biography:

> This habit of Harvey's has often been dismissed as an affectation or eccentricity, a gesture devoid of violence, but one man who knew him in Rome in the mid-1960s . . . considered Harvey a genuinely "dangerous clown." Asked why, the man said that once Harvey expressed his opinion in an argument by pulling a .45-caliber automatic from his desk drawer, pointing it between his listener's eyes at a distance of only two or three feet, and flipping the safety.

The goal of Operation Mongoose was straightforward: Lansdale wanted to see an army of rebel anticommunists march triumphantly into Cuba's capital, Havana, by October 1962. The trouble with this plan—and the Bay of Pigs and other failed covert operations before it—was that it presumed the existence of something that did not exist: a widespread and powerful resistance movement within Cuba. Lansdale had fallen into the trap that others had fallen into before, the feeling that there *just had* to be a resistance. Another problem was that Lansdale was better equipped to handle subtler forms of psychological and political war than he was to handle the commando-style operations Mongoose required. His experiences in Asia didn't translate to the Caribbean. In one of his proposed schemes (never carried out), Lansdale thought agents could convince the predominantly Catholic population of Cuba that the Second Coming was at hand and that Christ wanted Castro out.

As the resistance failed to materialize, even after the agency sent in agents to try to create one, the operational plans of Mongoose changed. No longer could the Counter-Insurgency Group hope to have a rebel force carried into Havana on the shoulders of the people, so instead they turned to a strategy of "boom and bang." The idea was to create chaos and havoc through sabotage and commando-style raids.

Over the next few years, dozens of teams took boats across the 90-mile stretch of water between Cuba and Florida and carried out raids on everything from bridges and railway lines to radio stations and government buildings. These actions did indeed create some chaos and confusion. However, they most certainly did not accomplish their ultimate goal, which was to bring Castro to his knees. So, while Harvey was overseeing these paramilitary actions, he also pursued the possibility of eliminating Castro directly.

In the fall of 1961, Bissell was still the chief of Clandestine Services. After being hauled on the carpet by the Kennedys (the president and his brother, Robert, the attorney general) for not doing enough to get rid of Castro, Bissell decided to bring one of his plans back to life. He spoke with Harvey about using the Mafia to assassinate Castro. They also discussed the "executive action" group that Harvey had set up within the agency at Bissell's behest. This group, code-named "ZR/RIFLE," was basically a hit squad, designed to carry out assassinations on call. On November 16, 1961, they discussed two possibilities—using either ZR/RIFLE or the Mafia to kill Castro.

By that time, Bissell wasn't long for the agency. When Helms replaced him in 1962, Harvey told Helms about both ZR/RIFLE and the Mafia plan. Helms didn't balk. In fact, in April 1962, he ordered Harvey to see if the Mafia idea might be workable. Harvey then contacted Rosselli, the Mafia connection the CIA had dealt with before, met with him in Miami and New York, and in late April 1962 gave him poison pills to be smuggled into Cuba and somehow administered to Castro. Although Rosselli reported in June that the pills and a hit squad had made it into Cuba, nothing of course ever came of the plan.

As it turned out, Harvey himself wasn't long for his job. He made his mistakes in the fall of 1962, during the Cuban Missile Crisis. During the summer, CIA agents within Cuba had reported that something was up, and U-2 flights over the island in early October found out just exactly what was going on. Despite all previous asssurances, the Soviets were getting ready to deploy nuclear missiles. This was an obvious, ominous threat to the United States. Kennedy demanded that the missiles not be deployed. Khrushchev refused. The two leaders went eyeball to eyeball. Finally, Khrushchev "blinked" and agreed to withdraw the nuclear weapons. It was during the two weeks of this incredibly intense drama that Harvey made his fatal errors.

First, in a meeting near the beginning of the crisis, Harvey rashly decided to inform the Kennedys that the crisis was their own fault. Second, after having been told to halt all operations against Cuba during the crisis, Harvey took it upon himself to make the distinction between operations and intelligence-gathering expeditions. He sent some agents in at night. When word of this got out, he was instantly removed from all Cuba-related operations. DCI McCone was quite ready to remove him from the CIA altogether, but Helms lobbied on Harvey's behalf, and in the end Harvey was posted to Rome as the station chief (the local CIA head). Harvey's replacement, Desmond FitzGerald, didn't halt the Castro assassination plans; he just took them in a new direction. FitzGerald was renowned in the agency for his love of gadgets and exotic spy-tech. He had a running battle over this with a fellow Clandestine Services officer, Sam Halpern, who wondered not only if these tricky devices would work, but also if they were necessary at all. This ongoing conflict wasn't restricted solely to Cuban operations. Once, when Halpern argued that an exotic communications gadget FitzGerald supported just wouldn't work, FitzGerald responded childishly, "If you don't like it you don't have to come to meetings anymore."

FitzGerald's favorite plans involved exploiting Castro's known love of scuba diving. One plot involved placing an unusual seashell under water, in an area where Castro loved to dive. The shell was rigged to explode when picked up. Halpern protested that the plan was uncontrollable—it might not be Castro who picked up the shell but some kid on a weekend dive. The other plot involved giving Castro scuba equipment with the breathing apparatus contaminated with a horrible fungus. Again, the problem was control—Castro might give the equipment to someone else. There was another problem as well: The trail of responsibility would lead directly to the CIA, leaving little chance for plausible denial.

FitzGerald also pursued a more straightforward plan for assassination. The CIA made contact with Rolando Cubela, a dissatisfied major in the Cuban army. Cubela, as the CIA knew, was disenchanted with the Castro regime and detested the heavy Soviet presence on the island. He agreed to assassinate Castro. Like FitzGerald, Cubela had a passion for exotic gadgets and weapons and requested these. The CIA's maker of "dirty tricks," the Technical Services Division, complied. On November 22, 1963, Cubela's case officer delivered to him a poison pen; it looked like a pen but could be used to inject poison into a victim. This was to be his method for assassinating Castro. It wasn't until after the meeting that the case officer heard the news: President Kennedy had been shot in Dallas.

The effort to oust Castro was never the same after that. The poison pen plan never came to anything, and while some further contact was made with Cubela—rifles were delivered to him, plans were made—nothing ever came of it.

One question that has remained unanswered over the years concerns the degree to which the Kennedy brothers knew of the Castro assassination plans. Did Jack or brother Bobby actually give the order to have Castro killed? While there is certainly no written record of that, it's not something that would likely be put in writing. What is clear, is that even if the president or his brother didn't actually give the order to kill Castro, they were well aware of what was going on and did nothing to stop it. It wasn't something they wanted to sign their names to, but it was something they wanted done.

In March 1964, Desmond FitzGerald, in his new capacity as Western Division Chief, visited the agency's station in Buenos Aires. He told some of the officers that if Jack Kennedy had lived, Castro would have been gotten rid of by the previous Christmas, and that President Johnson wasn't as gung-ho on fighting Castro as Kennedy had been. Indeed, Johnson wasn't as gung-ho. Early on, the agency tried testing the waters with him—someone asked what he thought about trying to eliminate Castro. When Johnson exploded with rage at the idea, the agency knew he'd be violently opposed to such plans. The idea was not mentioned again. On April 7 Johnson put an end to the boom and bang raids on Cuba. It wasn't be- cause Johnson wanted to go easy on Cuba. It was just that he had another country on his mind, another country he wanted the CIA to work on—Vietnam.

But the CIA's involvement in Vietnam didn't begin in 1965, when Johnson escalated the war by bombing North Vietnam and sending in more troops. The CIA had been active in the region for years. In fact, for several years they waged an entire war in secret in the country of Laos.

THE SECRET WAR IN LAOS

In 1953, the CIA again looked for a resistance movement in a communist country that didn't have one, then tried to set one up anyway. Again it was miserably disappointed. In this case, the country was a long way from the Iron Curtain—it was communist China. It was a type of failure that was becoming familiar. Agents infiltrated the country, only to be almost instantly rounded up and disposed of, and the lesson learned was that there was little hope for a rollback of communism in the countries that were already communist. The only places the CIA could be effective were those countries teetering on the edge.

So, the CIA's attention turned south of China, to the region known as Indochina, particularly to three countries: Vietnam, Cambodia and Laos. At that time, in 1953, the French were doing their best to hold on to Indochina, which had been a colonial holding since the early part of the century. France was up against assorted indigenous nationalist and communist forces, most notably the Viet Minh, led by the immensely popular Ho Chi Minh. France was losing. Defeat at the critical battle of Dien Bien Phu broke the French, and they pulled out of Indochina. The most immediate and apparent effect of the French pullout was the division, as set out by accords signed in Geneva in 1954, of Vietnam into two countries: North Vietnam—to be the domain of the Viet Minh—and South Vietnam—to be ruled by a U.S.-backed regime. But the French pullout affected the other countries in the area as well, especially Laos.

Laos is the landlocked nation of Indochina. It is surrounded by Vietnam to the east, Cambodia to the south, Thailand to the west, and Burma and China to the north. It is a mountainous country, heavily forested. Laos is shaped roughly like a hatchet, with the blade head at the top and the handle extending beneath it. The major river is the Mekong, which comes down out of the mountains of China, forms the border between Loas and Burma, then snakes southward through the heart of the country before forming the border with Thailand. It runs through the Laotian capital of Vietiane and remains the border between Thailand and Laos for most of its journey before flowing into Cambodia, then into Vietnam, and finally into the South China Sea.

Laos was unsettled by the French pullout. The government of Prince Souvanna Phouma remained in power, however, partly by adopting as neutral a position as possible. By 1958, the Pathet Lao, the communist rebel force in Laos, began to gain in strength and made some key advances. Instead of alienating them, Prince Souvanna decided to try to include the Pathet Lao in the power structure. As was shown in Iran and Guatemala, however, whenever a government makes attempts to bring communists into the government, the United States is displeased. Laos was no exception. The United States put its support behind a group of right-wing generals and Souvanna was ousted. Phoumi Nosavan, a general, was put in Souvanna's place as the leader of the country.

Not everyone in Laos was pleased with this turn of events. Many Laotians resented the rather obvious meddling of the United States in their internal affairs. In 1960 there was a coup, led by 25-year-old army captain Kong Lae, which sent Nosavan out of office. Instead of assuming power himself, though, Kong Lae asked Souvanna to return and form a government.

The United States, however, had not given up on Nosavan. Despite the strong urging of the U.S. ambassador to Laos, who suggested that the United States should promote and support a coalition government of Souvanna, Nosavan and Kong Lae, the CIA opted to continue its support for Nosavan. They were convinced Nosavan could go it alone. Meanwhile, Souvanna, back in power with the support of Kong Lae, repeatedly requested aid from the United States. The United

States said they would give the aid, but only if Souvanna broke off all relations with the communist Pathet Lao. Souvanna felt he couldn't do it, so the United States turned down his request for aid. Souvanna then did what other leaders in his position have done: He turned to the Soviets for help. When the Soviets agreed to the request, the United States stepped up its support for Nosavan. Nosavan and his men marched on Vientiane, retook it, and ousted Souvanna and Kong Lae. Kong fled to the hills and joined ranks with the Pathet Lao, who, strengthened by Kong's allegiance, continued to make advances.

When President Kennedy took office in January 1961, he went on a campaign to "Save Laos." He ordered the Seventh Fleet into the region, went on TV to make his case to the American public and the world, and warned the Pathet Lao to back off from the capital of Vientiane. Kennedy's campaign prompted a conference in Geneva, which in turn produced a compromise that seemed acceptable. Souvanna, representing his own neutralist interests and those of the Pathet Lao, would form a coalition government with Nosavan.

This satisfied the United States. It did not, however, satisfy Nosavan, who, much to the surprise and chagrin of the United States, vowed to continue fighting. He assumed he would continue to receive the backing of the CIA as he had in the past. He was wrong. DCI McCone was outraged, and in response he ordered every CIA officer out of the country. The United States would not back Nosavan on what appeared to be a foolhardy and unpromising campaign. Nosavan was undaunted and soldiered on. He made a crucial tactical and strategic error, however. He tried to confront the communists head on, in an offensive in the heart of Pathet Lao-controlled country. He was soundly defeated.

Brought to his senses as it were, Nosavan finally gave in and agreed to a three-party coalition of himself, Souvanna and the Pathet Lao. Part of the agreement noted, however, that the United States would withdraw its advisors to Nosavan. At the same time the North Vietnamese, who had been aiding the Pathet Lao, would withdraw their support as well. Things didn't work out that way. The North Vietnamese did not leave; the coalition prospects crumbled; Kong Lae and the Pathet Lao continued their battle from the hills; and in Vientiane, Nosavan held onto his tentative control.

The CIA, which had withdrawn from the country in response to Nosavan going rogue, returned now in full force. From here on in, the CIA waged a secret war against the Pathet Lao.

For many in the agency, this was the perfect kind of covert operation. Operating on a budget of $70 million, the CIA went into the hills surrounding the region known as the Plain of Jars and recruited Meo tribesmen. The Meo had lived in the hills, leading a simple life, for centuries. All that would change suddenly and irrevocably. The CIA trained these hill people and turned them into a formidable secret army. While the CIA did have some advisors in the field, most of the training and command of the forces was conducted by local leaders and contract employees. The leader of the force was General Vang Pao, a popular and influential figure.

The beauty of the operation, as far as the CIA was concerned, was that it didn't take a lot of manpower on the agency's part; there were never more than 30 or 40 CIA

An abandoned secret CIA base hidden high in the hills of Laos. [Credit: UPI/ Bettmann Newsphotos]

officers in Vientiane. Best of all, of course, the operation was successful. Although the Meo tribesmen didn't defeat the Pathet Lao, they did harass them and keep them from assuming control. What began as a small operation involving a few teams of Meo grew until the Meo army had more than 30,000 troops. As the war in Vietnam progressed, the Meos under Vang Pao not only staved off the Pathet Lao, they also found the time to harrass North Vietnamese and Viet Cong movement on the Ho Chi Minh trail. This important trail, which snaked through part of Laos, was North Vietnam's supply route to the south.

One of the CIA's main assets in waging this secret war was a company it owned, an airline called Air America. Air America was a *proprietary company* of the agency's. In many ways proprietaries are cover companies. An agent in Hong Kong can say he or she works for the Pan Pacific Import/ Export Company when in fact he or she works for the CIA. But Air America offered more than that, for as an airline, it could also offer concrete logistical support to operations. On the surface it was a legitimate business, ferrying cargo and passengers here and there around the world. At the same time, however, it was also airlifting arms and supplies to assorted secret armies all over the map.

Before its use in Laos, Air America had earned its wings in Tibet. In 1959, the exiled religious leader of Tibet, the Dalai Lama, angered over his nation's occupation by Chinese troops, led a popular uprising. It didn't last long. As Peking reasserted control over the region, the Dalai Lama and his men escaped into India. The CIA then got behind the Dalai Lama. Agents trained his troops, the fearsome Khambu horsemen, even bringing some of them to Camp Hale in Colorado for advanced training. Then, using Air America to ferry men and supplies, the CIA-backed Tibetans began a series of attacks on the Chinese occupying force. The CIA promised the Dalai Lama that it would put him back on the throne in Lhasa, the Tibetan capital. In retrospect, however, it seems likely that all the CIA ever intended for the operation was to be a particularly annoying thorn in the side of the Chinese.

The operation continued throughout much of the 1960s, but by the end of the decade the CIA was withdrawing its support for the Dalai Lama. Now, several decades since the Dalai Lama was forced into exile, he is still alive and still in exile. The Chinese still occupy Tibet. Lhasa, once a fabled city at the top of the world, now looks as drab and colorless as any Chinese provincial town. The conflict also remains. In the fall of 1987, riots surrounding a prayer festival left scores of Tibetans dead.

In many ways the operation in Laos followed a similar course—an initial rush of enthusiasm and involvement that gradually faded. It wasn't just that the war in Vietnam took precedence over the Laotian operation—it was that the war in Vietnam affected events in Laos. As the war went in Vietnam, so it did in Laos, and when the tide turned in the favor of the North Vietnamese and Viet Cong, the tide turned against the Meo tribesmen. When the United States pulled its troops out of Vietnam in 1973, the CIA withdrew its support from Laos, and the Meo army collapsed.

The CIA has often been criticized for its use of the Meo tribesmen, both for the way it recruited and exploited them and also for the way it abandoned them. When the communists eventually came to power in Laos, the Meo no longer had a country. Because of their having been tainted by collaboration with the United States, and especially the CIA, they were considered to be enemies. The CIA did manage to get a few of the Meo to safety in the United States—leader Vang Pao ended up in Missoula, Montana—but most were not so lucky. In the early 1960s, when the secret war began, there were 250,000 Meo in Laos. In 1975, when the communists assumed control of Laos, the remaining Meo fled into Thailand. There were only 10,000 of them left.

VIETNAM

The division of Vietnam into North and South by the Geneva Accords of 1954 was an attempt both to placate and satisfy Ho Chi Minh and to give the anticommunists time to regroup. In 1953, while the Viet Minh battled the French and forced them out, there was a fear that Ho Chi Minh was about to overrun the whole region. For one thing, he was an immensely popular leader. Even Eisenhower later wrote, "I have never talked or corresponded with a person knowledgeable in Indochinese affairs who did not agree that had elections been held as of the time of the fighting, possibly 80 percent of the population would have voted for Ho Chi Minh."

Ho's widespread popularity notwithstanding, roughly 800,000 people did flee the North for the South. They fled for a variety of reasons. For one thing, many of them were Catholics, and Catholics were in power in the South while they were oppressed in the North (to this day Catholics continue to be ostracized and oppressed in Vietnam—the majority of those Vietnamese who escaped the country by boat in the 1970s and 1980s were Catholic). Many who left the North were also fleeing the chaos created by a disastrously ill-conceived land reform program that Ho tried to impose on the countryside. And they also left because the CIA waged a very effective propaganda war of disinformation and dirty tricks.

By 1955, the U.S.-backed leader of the South, Ngo Dinh Diem, had marshaled his forces and consolidated his power. The CIA worked closely with Diem, even closer with Diem's brother, Ngo Dinh Nhu. The Saigon station chief during this time (1959-1962) was William Colby, a man who would later become DCI. The CIA's main programs in those early years of American involvement in Vietnam were the Strategic Hamlets Program and arming the hill tribesmen of Vietnam. These tribesmen, the Montagnards, were related to the Meo in Laos.

The strategic hamlets were intended to be strongholds against the Viet Cong, the North-sponsored communist rebels working in the South. Unfortunately, under Nhu, the strategic hamlets became little more than concentration camps.

By arming and training the Montagnards, the CIA hoped to recreate its success in Laos with the Meo. They wanted another clandestine army that could fight a secret war for them in the jungles.

By the early 1960s, the U.S. relationship with Diem was souring. Diem's regime was characterized by brutality and corruption. While the United States and the CIA have learned to live with this in other governments before and since, in the case of Diem the situation was so bad that it was weakening his grip on the nation. The worst was that Diem wasn't merely Catholic, he was actively anti-Buddhist. Buddhism is a religion based on the teachings of Buddha, a religious leader who lived in India about 500 B.C. It is the major religion of much of Asia. In South Vietnam, a country where the majority of the population was Buddhist, Diem's anti-Buddhism clearly spelled trouble. Diem's goons went so far as to actively harass Buddhists and wreck their temples. The horrifying manner one Buddhist monk chose to protest this oppression was seen in newspaper photos around the world. He sat down in the middle of a public thoroughfare, doused himself with gasoline and set himself on fire.

This was too much for many to take. The fear was that Diem would be swept out by religious fervor and a popular uprising. His support in the U.S. government withered, and in 1963, the Kennedy administration contributed—by not doing anything to stop it—to a coup that removed Diem from office. Not everyone agreed with the coup. DCI McCone voiced his objections to President Kennedy: "My precise words to the President, and I remember them very clearly, was that, 'Mr. President, if I was manager of a baseball team, [and] I had one pitcher, I'd keep him in the box whether he was a good pitcher or not.'" Kennedy was not swayed, and Diem was out.

Shortly after Diem was deposed, he and his brother Nhu were executed. Kennedy, who perhaps had not considered that this would be the final result of the coup, was sitting in the Cabinet Room of the White House with his advisors when the news of Diem's and Nhu's murder came in. According to one of the advisors present, "Kennedy leaped to his feat and rushed from the room with a look of shock and dismay on his face which I had never seen before."

It didn't take long before the United States had put new people in power in South Vietnam, and over the years there

An American military advisor shown with two South Vietnamese infantrymen in 1964. CIA advisors, not likely to be photographed, had been in the country, organizing a secret war, for years. [Courtesy Shelby L. Stanton Collection]

was a succession from Nguyen Khanh through Nguyen Cao Ky, to Nguyen Van Thieu. While the various leaders that followed Diem were probably no less corrupt than he had been, they were easily controlled puppets of the United States with the good sense to do as they were told.

In 1964, American ships reported being fired upon by North Vietnamese attack vessels in international waters in the Gulf of Tonkin, off the coast of North Vietnam. This incident was seized upon by the Johnson administration as an excuse to escalate American involvement in Vietnam, which, until that time, had been limited to an advisory capacity. In February 1965 Johnson began the bombing of North Vietnam, and by that summer, Johnson had sent American troops into the field, making Vietnam an American war.

When the American military landed in Vietnam, the role of the CIA was largely overshadowed. Before 1965, the time when the conflict really became a full-scale war, the CIA had been engaging in many covert actions against the communist government of Hanoi (the North Vietnamese capital). There were fairly straightforward commando raids on assorted installations; indeed, the North Vietnamese gunboats involved in the Gulf of Tonkin incident are now believed to have been responding to just such a commando raid. There were also more cunning plots. An attempt was made to poison the police chief of Hanoi with a contaminated bottle of apricot brandy, and one plan, never attempted, called for the kidnapping of the entire North Vietnamese government.

William Colby, who had been promoted and moved since his earlier days in Vietnam, returned to Saigon (the South Vietnamese capital) in 1968 when his expertise was required. The operation he was to oversee was one that would dominate the CIA's actions during the war in Vietnam—the Phoenix program. Colby maintains that it was an intelligence gathering operation, designed to infiltrate the Viet Cong. Frank Snepp maintains otherwise.

Snepp is the author of *Decent Interval*, a book about the last days of the CIA in Vietnam and the fall of Saigon. Snepp, who was a senior CIA officer in Saigon during the war, says that the Phoenix program was essentially an assassination program. The Phoenix teams—primarily Vietnamese operatives—were supposed to go into the countryside and identify the Viet Cong. Then, Provincial Reconnaissance Units (the notorious PRUs) were to find the Viet Cong and cart them off for interrogation. However, they were often just simply shot instead. The trouble with the Phoenix program, though, wasn't so much that Viet Cong were being killed—killing the enemy is, after all, part of war—but that there was no real guarantee that all the people being killed were Viet Cong. It is reported that Phoenix teams would descend on a hut with an accused Viet Cong inside, slaughter all the occupants, and *then* report that they were all Viet Cong.

Colby conceded that Phoenix killed over 20,000 suspected Viet Cong (some estimates put the number at over 40,000) and that there were some excesses. Despite those excesses,

Colby continued to argue, even after the war, that Phoenix had been a success. In his opinion, the reason the North Vietnamese had to send down their own army to win the war was because the Viet Cong had been all but eliminated by Phoenix.

The CIA did do other work in Vietnam besides Phoenix. The agency made some attempts at traditional spying, but these attempts were at first half-hearted. At the time of the Tet Offensive in early 1968, when the Viet Cong and North Vietnamese army mounted an unsettling surprise attack throughout the country, the United States had only one high-level spy in the enemy camp. At the same time, it was estimated that the North Vietnamese had 40,000 spies at all levels throughout Vietnam. The CIA then quickly stepped up its attempts to infiltrate North Vietnam. This was almost impossible. A common observation in the CIA at that time was that if Russia was hard to penetrate, China was even harder, and North Korea harder still (it was said that Pyongyang, the capital of North Korea, was a blank spot on the CIA's map). Hanoi was another blank spot and remained that way throughout the war.

The CIA became involved in a controversy during the war that continues to this day. It had to do with estimates of the enemy's number of troops. The military estimated that there were 270,000 troops on the other side. But a CIA analyst, Sam Adams, working from what he considered to be much more reliable figures, estimated that there were 500,000 enemy troops—roughly twice as many. The military steadfastly refused to accept Adams's figure. Adams believed the military was set on the lower figure because it allowed them to prove they were winning the war; suddenly saying there were twice as many Viet Cong and North Vietnamese in the field would not help their cause one bit.

While Adams finally did get the military to use his figures, he was not a happy man. He accused Helms, who had been promoted to DCI during the war, of blocking his efforts. He went so far as to go over Helms's head and try to have him fired. And he continued to charge General Westmoreland, the commander of American forces in Vietnam, among others, with suppressing his figures. This charge of Adams's against Westmoreland surfaced again in a CBS documentary years later. Westmoreland sued the producer of the documentary, George Crile, and others for libel and won.

Of course, one reason the military had been reluctant to use CIA figures was that the military didn't trust the CIA. It was well known throughout the U.S. government that the CIA simply didn't think the United States could win a conventional land war in Vietnam. The feeling around the CIA was that the United States was caught in a no-man's-land of compromise between a small war and a big war. The CIA thought the United States should do one of two things. The first was to do something like the CIA was doing in Laos (which, as one observer noted, for the same results was costing the CIA for a *year* what the military was spending *each day* in Vietnam). The second was to commit fully, which would have meant still more troops and all-out bombing of North Vietnam. The CIA was right, of course, but at that time it was too late to go back to a secret war, and the war was already too unpopular to be allowed to grow.

The harshest criticism of the agency's role in Vietnam, and the one leveled by former agent Snepp in *Decent Interval*, was not over the Phoenix program but over how the agency handled its withdrawal from the country. When American troops pulled out in 1973, the CIA remained. Agency officers stayed on until April 30, 1975, when the North Vietnamese army entered Saigon and the U.S. embassy had to be evacuated. The CIA's great crime, so far as Snepp and others are concerned, was its abandonment of the numerous South Vietnamese agents it had recruited and used. As with the Meo in Laos, the people who had done most of the work and most of the fighting were left behind.

The final betrayal came when the North Vietnamese entered the U.S. embassy and found that the files containing the names of the agents who had worked for the United States had not been destroyed. Those men and women did not live long.

MCCONE, RABORN AND HELMS

The men who serve as DCI always serve one boss, the president. The success or failure of these men as DCIs often simply reflects their relationship with the men they serve. One reason Allen Dulles was such an effective DCI was that he had a good working relationship with Eisenhower and, for a time, with Kennedy. Dulles lost his job because of the Bay of Pigs and because he had lost Kennedy's confidence.

The man Kennedy finally settled on as a replacement for Dulles was an outsider, John McCone. McCone certainly had the necessary credentials—he had been chairman of the Atomic Energy Commission. But he was also chosen because he was politically correct. He was a conservative Republican and Kennedy needed to shore up his support among this group.

McCone had, according to some, a rather brusque and haughty manner, but he was intelligent and shrewd. His shrewdness paid off early. After the Bay of Pigs, the President's Foreign Intelligence Advisory Board (PFIAB) suggested that the CIA be dismantled to a degree, with the office of DCI to be brought into the White House where a close eye could be kept on the DCI and the agency could be kept on a short leash. McCone didn't want to let that happen, and so the day he took office, he smartly moved into the un-painted DCI office at the new CIA headquarters at Langley instead of into the White House. The effort to bring the DCI into the White House eventually faded away.

McCone was generally good at fighting for what he wanted and getting it, although the major battle he fought was one he lost. When McCone took office, the first American reconnaissance satellite programs, Discoverer and Samos, were just becoming fully operative. McCone knew that spy satellites would be the future of espionage, and so he struggled hard to have the CIA keep control of the programs. His battle was with the Air Force, which wanted the CIA relegated to an advisory role. To shore up his position, McCone created a new directorate within the CIA, the Directorate of Science and Technology, which was to concentrate primarily on the building and operation of high-flying spies. McCone eventually lost the battle. The Air Force's top secret National Reconnaissance Office now runs the $3 to $5 billion a year satellite program. But, because of his efforts, the CIA didn't suffer the loss it might have, and the agency is still closely involved with the development and running of the satellite spies.

The crucial part of McCone's tenure, however, was his relationship with the presidents he served. Initially his relationship with Kennedy was excellent, but eventually it soured. Ironically, McCone lost Kennedy's ear over something that should be remembered as one of his greater achievements—the Cuban Missile Crisis. McCone had gone against the grain as early as August 1962, by saying that the evidence presented to him strongly suggested the Soviets were about to deploy nuclear missiles on Cuba. Everyone else said no: *The Soviets wouldn't be that foolhardy.* McCone didn't force his opinion, but it was registered, and he stayed close to the situation. When he turned out to be right, his foresight was duly noted. The trouble was, McCone mentioned how smart he'd been too often. No one, including a president, likes to hear "I told you so." McGeorge Bundy, a top Kennedy advisor, reportedly once said to a CIA man, "I'm so tired of listening to McCone say he was right I never want to hear it again." Annoyed with McCone, Kennedy began tapering off the DCI's access to the Oval Office, access that in many ways defines the success or failure of a DCI's tenure.

Immediately after Kennedy's assassination, McCone became a frequent visitor to the Oval Office, briefing President Johnson on a variety of subjects. Eventually, though, he lost Johnson's ear as well. The problem this time had to do with Vietnam. Like many in the CIA, McCone was convinced that the United States could not win a limited land war. He felt U.S. involvement had to be all or nothing—either bomb the hell out of North Vietnam and fully commit, or scale it way back. That was not a popular opinion at the time, and McCone and Johnson split over it. So far as Johnson was concerned, McCone was "off the team," he was "out of the loop." For McCone, the straw that broke the camel's back came when he tried, unsuccessfully, to get Johnson to read the CIA's *Annual Survey of Soviet Intentions and Capabilities.* "When I can't even get the President to read the summaries, it's time for me to leave." And so he did.

Johnson conducted a long, hard search for a replacement for McCone. The man he finally settled on as the new DCI was Admiral William F. Raborn, a fellow Texan and key supporter during Johnson's 1964 presidential campaign. Raborn was most noted for having managed the program that built the Navy's submarine-launched missile, the Polaris. It was hoped that he could bring his managerial expertise to the CIA. Raborn was sworn in at the White House on April 28, 1965. He lasted barely a year.

That Raborn was an outsider wasn't the real problem— CIA career men had tolerated, even worked well for, outsiders in the past. The problem was that he knew very little about world affairs and even less about intelligence. After a talk on management technique to agency officers, in which Raborn gave a confusing account of how he'd handled the Polaris program, one officer remarked, "I'm beginning to wonder if Polaris really works."

In his biography of Richard Helms, Thomas Powers recounts a telling story of how ill-suited Raborn was for the job:

> One of the Admiral's worst blunders came at a morning staff meeting where he opened the discussion with a remark that he'd just read something interesting about the Russians and the Chinese not getting along. There was dead silence around the table . . . a dozen top CIA officials stonyfaced.
>
> "No, listen, fellows, this is really important." He turned to Ray Cline, the Deputy Director for Intelligence, and said, "I want you to do a paper on this."
>
> Ray Cline had been studying the Sino–Soviet split . . . since . . . 1956. Perhaps no other subject had been so relentlessly analyzed . . . in the previous ten years. They had been over and *over* this. . . Raborn had just announced that the world was round. Cline said politely that this matter had already been the subject of a good deal of study and there was, truly, no need of a special paper at this time.
>
> But Raborn persisted. . . grew pugnacious. "You're not taking this seriously. I want you to send me up your papers on this. I want to see all these studies."

Cline's patience broke. "Well, what do you want me to use," he snapped, "a *wheelbarrow*?"

When Johnson announced that Raborn was stepping down as DCI, he tried to make it look as if he had intended right from the start that Raborn would be in the office only for a year; he wanted it to appear that his appointment had been a temporary one, to fill the gap until a long-term choice was made. In truth, Johnson had simply made a mistake with Raborn.

For Raborn's successor, Johnson decided against another long, involved search and looked within the agency, to a man who had been with the CIA from the beginning. He chose someone who would become the first career pro to reach the office of DCI—Richard Helms.

Helms was sworn in as the new DCI on June 30, 1966. In his six-year tenure as DCI, Helms would be primarily concerned with the war in Vietnam, as was the entire U.S. government. But Vietnam, as it happened, is not what Helms is remembered for.

President Lyndon Johnson (center) announces the departure of Admiral William F. Raborn (left) as the Director of Central Intelligence, and the selection of Richard Helms (right) to succeed him. The smiles belie the fact that Raborn's appointment as DCI was a mistake and his tenure was mercifully short. [Credit: UPI/ Bettmann Newsphotos]

7

RICHARD HELMS:
FROM CHILE TO WATERGATE

When Richard Helms was working for the CIA in the 1950s, he was like one of those fathers on a TV sitcom of that period who would wear a boring suit, drive a boring car, and go off each day to an unnamed, probably boring job. Helms wore the suit and drove the car because his job was anything *but* boring. He didn't simply accept such anonymity, he sought it out. To him, the very essence of operating a successful spy agency was to keep its profile low. The last thing a spy or spy agency would want would be to call attention to itself.

It's ironic, then, that when the spotlight was shone on the CIA, it would focus on the years that Helms was DCI. Certainly, there would be investigations into operations that occurred before Helms was DCI—the Castro assassination plans, for example—but no person would be as devastated by the investigations and their aftermath as Helms. Imagine his dismay—a man who, if he had to be thought of at all by the public, would like to have been remembered as a clear-thinking, levelheaded, hardworking intelligence professional, and as the first DCI to have risen through the ranks. Instead, he is remembered as the only DCI in history to be convicted of a crime.

A further irony—the operation that was the undoing of Helms was not the kind of operation that Helms was particularly enthusiastic about. Helms liked penetrating other nations, recruiting and running agents. The operation that eventually got him into trouble was a covert attempt to meddle in the democratic elections of another nation—Chile.

CHILE

I don't see why we need to stand by and watch a country go Communist due to the irresponsibility of its own people.

—Henry Kissinger, June 27,
1970, at a secret White House
meeting regarding Chile
(Quoted in Thomas Powers'
*The Man Who Kept the
Secrets: Richard Helms and the CIA*)

The CIA was active throughout Latin America in the 1960s. When Peru was having some difficulty with marauding bands of rebels, it asked the United States for help. The CIA went in, trained an elite corp in techniques used to fight the rebels, and quickly routed the troublemakers. The crack team the agency created was so good, in fact, that the Peruvian government was afraid of it and had it disbanded.

In 1965, Ché Guevara, famous revolutionary and close comrade of Castro's, disappeared from Cuba. He was finally tracked to the hills of Bolivia where in 1967, he was attempting to foment revolution. When Helms was finally convinced that Ché was indeed there, he lent the agency's assistance to the Bolivian military, and the revolutionary was ferreted out of the jungle. The Bolivians wanted to execute Ché, but the CIA wanted his life to be spared—not necessarily for humanitarian reasons, but because the agency didn't want him to become a martyr. The Bolivians won the argument and Ché was killed.

There was other work for the CIA throughout Latin America during this period. It helped set up a government run by the military in Brazil in 1964 and helped fight the Tupamaros, urban guerillas, in Uruguay, from 1968 to 1973 (a struggle that turned Uruguay from a democracy into a military dictatorship). But the greatest amount of time and money was spent in Chile.

Kennedy had picked Chile as the counterpoint to Cuba. It would be the standard-bearer for democracy in Latin America. It was a good choice, because the country had a tradition of democracy dating back to the 19th century. Its history was *not* simply a string of coups and countercoups like those in other countries of the region.

The first major U.S. involvement in Chile came during the country's presidential elections in 1964. The reason the agency became involved was the candidacy of Salvador Allende. Allende, a doctor, was a communist who vowed to nationalize much of the country's industry if elected. The trouble with this plan was that several American companies had invested rather heavily in Chile, including Anaconda (which operated much of Chile's lucrative copper industry) and ITT. They had invested partly because they had been given a guarantee by Kennedy and others that their holdings would never fall prey to nationalization.

The only candidate who stood a chance to beat Allende was Eduardo Frei of the Christian Democrats, and so the CIA underwrote roughly half of his campaign (something Frei was apparently unaware of). The CIA felt this move was justified by the fact that Allende was reportedly receiving financial support from the Soviets. The CIA also poured vast amounts of money into straightforward propaganda, plastering the capital, Santiago, with posters showing Allende with Castro and Soviet tanks rolling down the streets. As was the case with the CIA's meddling in the Italian elections years before, it's hard to say what they actually accomplished and how much of the result was simply due to the will of the Chilean people. In any event, Frei won.

Six years later, however, when the time for elections came around again in 1970, the problem was still there—Allende was running for office again. This time, as far as the United States was concerned, the problem was actually worse, for it looked as if Allende would win. For one thing, the only man who stood a strong chance of beating Allende was Frei, and he was constitutionally unable to run for reelection.

As far as American business interests were concerned, the fact that Frei wasn't going to run again wasn't such a bad thing. Frei was a fairly liberal man, and while not nearly as leftist as Allende, he had instituted many reforms and had promised eventual nationalization of several of Chile's industries. The captains of American industry who had investments in Chile were not pleased with such notions and were happy to see Frei go.

In the 1964 elections, the CIA had done its work alone, but this time American business interests wanted more direct involvement. They even chose the candidate they wanted to back—staunch ultra-conservative, "right-winger" Jorge Alessandri.

One man caught in the middle of all this was the American ambassador to Chile, Edward Korry. Korry was as opposed to Allende as anyone could be, but he did not think backing Alessandri was a good idea at all. He felt that supporting Alessandri, who was little more than a candidate of the rich vowing to undo all of Frei's reforms, would simply drive the country further into Allende's camp.

The Business Group for Latin America was the name given to the loose collection of corporations that wanted to block Allende and put Alessandri in. This group had a great deal of influence in Washington. One of the companies involved was Pepsi, and Richard Nixon, who was president at this time, had worked at Pepsi. One of his friends now headed the company. ITT was involved, and John McCone, former DCI, was a major figure at ITT.

This high-level lobbying power and Kissinger's "I don't see why we need to stand by and watch a country go Communist due to the irresponsibility of its own people" statement notwithstanding, the decision was made *not* to back Alessandri but simply to run an anti-Allende campaign. The funds made available, $500,000, were meager compared to the huge investment back in 1964. There was, frankly, little chance of success. For one thing, it's hard to run a campaign *against* someone without offering an alternative. So, undeterred by the setback, the business group gave the CIA $700,000 to spend in support of Alessandri. This enraged Korry, who had several run-ins over it with the CIA's Santiago station chief, Henry Heckscher.

The secret funding did perhaps hurt Allende's campaign and help Alessandri's, but it wasn't enough. When the votes were tallied on September 4, 1970, Allende had emerged with a narrow victory. He had 36.3 percent of the vote to Alessandri's 34.9 percent. What spelled defeat for Alessandri was an agreement made before the election between Allende and the third candidate, Radomiro Tomic, a Christian Democrat who received 27.8 percent of the vote. In an effort to make sure that Alessandri would not become president, they agreed that the one with the most votes would get the other's support.

The Nixon administration panicked. Helms was called to a meeting at the White House on September 15, 1970, where the following points were jotted down:

One in ten chance perhaps, but save Chile!
Worth spending
Not concerned risks involved
No involvement of embassy
$10,000,000 available, more if necessary
Full-time job—best men we have
Game plan
Make the economy scream
48 hours for plan of action

There was a little time between the election and Allende's inauguration. The first idea then was to somehow keep Allende from taking office. One rather convoluted plan, which Ambassador Korry supported, involved some tricky footwork that would step around the Chilean constitution, force another election, and allow Frei to run again.

There was also something in the wind about a possible coup attempt. The commander of the Chilean armed forces,

General Rene Schneider, was categorically opposed: He had vowed to uphold the constitution and as Allende had been elected democratically, that was enough for him. So, word was put out that $50,000 was available for anyone who would kidnap Schneider. There were three attempts. The first two—in which the CIA was slightly involved—were bungled horribly. The third attempt, on October 23, 1970—for which the CIA disclaims any responsibility—was, paradoxically, both a success and a failure. Schneider was successfully kidnapped, but he was wounded during abduction and died several days later. Even with Schneider out of the picture, however, no coup took place.

Over the next three years, Allende followed through on his campaign promises, socializing the government and nationalizing major industries. The CIA also followed through on some of its promises, spending $8 million from 1970 to 1973 to destabilize Allende. Millions were channeled into the anti-Allende newspaper El Mercurio; more money was given to both the Christian Democrats and the right-wing National Party. Even American journalists were drawn in. Some were commissioned by the CIA to write anti-Allende slanted pieces. It is said that Time, which was going to run a piece by its Santiago correspondent reporting that Allende was no Soviet puppet, was persuaded to change the article and toe the CIA line.

By 1973 the Chilean economy was in shambles; there were food shortages and widespread strikes. This may have been partly because of CIA manipulation—Nixon had, after all, requested that the economy be made to scream. But it was mostly due to Allende's mismanagement and the tendency of major corporations to take their money and run from any country where industries were nationalized.

On September 11, 1973, there was a successful coup against the Allende government led by General Augusto Pinochet Ugarte. In the aftermath of the bloody fighting around the Presidential Palace, Allende's body was found. The official report was that he committed suicide, although subsequent reports have made that seem highly unlikely.

The last known photograph of Chilean President Salvador Allende, shown (center, with glasses) on the day of the coup. [Credit: UPI/Bettmann Newsphotos]

To this day there has been no direct connection established between the CIA and this coup. In all likelihood the CIA did not initiate or orchestrate the coup. The agency may have known of it in advance and may even have provided some advice and support, but it was probably not a "CIA coup."

Chile, once the standard-bearer for democracy in Latin America, is now the standard-bearer for human rights abuses and lack of freedom. Pinochet's regime has been characterized by death squads, torture, arbitrary "disappearances" and the infamous DINA, one of the most notorious security services in the world—one that the CIA has, on occasion, worked with. Through DINA, Pinochet effectively crushed all resistance, even reaching into the United States to kill Orlando Letelier, former Allende ambassador to the United States, with a car bomb. Only in the 1980s did any opposition begin to reemerge in Chile. Now, however, driven by years of desperation, the opposition is more radical and more Marxist than it ever was before.

Helms's trouble with the Chilean operation began before the coup. Secret memoranda were leaked and investigative articles were written. There was the general idea in the air in Washington that the CIA and some American corporations had meddled in the 1970 Chilean elections. There was nothing concrete, however, and nothing actually caught up with Helms until several years later, after he had been removed from the office of DCI because of a completely different scandal.

HELMS AND NIXON

Nixon had not liked the CIA and he had not warmed to Richard Helms. He had not given Helms his confidence; at times he would not even see him. Helms had often been reduced to leaving him notes at National Security Council meetings. He would arrive early. There was a yellow legal pad and sharpened pencil before every chair. Helms would go to Nixon's chair at the head of the table and write him a note on the yellow pad, asking to see him.

—Thomas Powers, *The Man Who Kept the Secrets*

Helms had seen this happen before, with other DCIs before him. He had seen Dulles lose Kennedy's confidence after the Bay of Pigs. He had seen McCone shut out of Kennedy's inner circle for harping on his foresight about the Cuban Missile Crisis, then shut out of Johnson's for his views on Vietnam. In the case of Helms and Nixon, however, there was no single event or action, no turning point that excluded him—that would come much later, at the very end of Helms's tenure. It wasn't that Nixon distrusted Helms himself, it was a matter of Nixon not trusting the CIA. It was a distrust that was, in retrospect, part of a larger, pervasive suspicion on Nixon's part of almost everything and everyone around him.

This is not to say that Helms didn't disappoint Nixon on occasion. When Nixon came to the Oval Office in January 1969, he was bent on changing things. He wanted his own people in; he wanted to shake things up. Nixon wanted to wipe the slate clean and start again, with an organization he felt would be loyal to him. The CIA and American intelligence in general were things that Nixon was always tinkering with.

After the 1968 election, Nixon decided that Helms would stay on as DCI, but he wanted to see some changes in the intelligence community. At that point, the community had become a bureaucracy out of control, expanding willy-nilly. And it was not working the way it was supposed to. The DCI was intended to be the head of the entire intelligence community. In practice, however, the power resided where the money did—in the Pentagon. This is how Helms disappointed Nixon. Nixon wanted the intelligence community brought under control. To do this, he tried to reorganize and boost the DCI's power, but Helms was unable to follow through on it. Helms tried to review the impenetrable National Security Agency but came up against a brick wall. One internal CIA report written for him concluded that too much intelligence was being collected. Even though this conformed to Helms's personal feelings—he preferred human spies to technical ones—the report ruffled too many feathers. It ended up being suppressed and its author was exiled to the Office of Training.

Helms did manage to quash one enormously expensive, potential white-elephant project of the Pentagon's—the Manned Orbiting Laboratory (MOL). At a cost of billions, MOL was supposed to put human spies in space, for truly no other discernible purpose than to repair spy equipment if it should fail. But, beyond that, Helms was never able to rein in the bureaucracy and take control.

It wasn't for lack of trying that Helms didn't accomplish what Nixon had asked of him. Helms believed that it was the duty of the CIA in general, and the DCI in particular, to serve the president and do his bidding. It was generally felt that if the president asks for it, then it's okay, even if its legality is a little doubtful. Such bowing to presidential authority led the CIA to break one of the most basic rules of its existence.

There is a sharp division between the CIA and the FBI: The FBI is allowed to conduct domestic espionage operations; the CIA is not. This reflects the concern that dates back to Truman's initial hesitancy over even creating the CIA—he didn't want America to have a secret police, a Gestapo. Over the years, some latitude was given the CIA. It was allowed, for example, to spy on foreign nationals as part of overseas investigations. In the 1960s, however, it began to spy on Americans at home.

The domestic spying program actually began with Johnson, who suspected that there was some conspiracy behind the antiwar movement—he was sure it was the work of international communists. He asked Helms to prepare a report on the matter. Helms thought, naturally, that this would be a job for the FBI, but J. Edgar Hoover insisted that the bureau did not do such analysis, that all his people did was collect information. Much of the information the FBI gathered was completely unsubstantiated and amounted to little more than rumor—there's a secret guerilla training base in Colorado; radicals plan to contaminate the New York City water supply with LSD; and so on. Helms and the CIA then had the job of sorting through the available information and figuring out what was going on.

The result was a report delivered to Johnson in November 1967. It concluded that the antiwar movement was part of a worldwide trend of student protest, but that the activity in the United States was American born and bred. The report stated clearly that there was no international communist conspiracy behind it. Johnson and his secretary of state, Dean Rusk, were appalled. They didn't accept the report and ordered Helms to prepare a new one. This is a fact of life for the CIA. If the analysis the agency gives doesn't conform to what the powers that be want to hear, it must be gone over again and again until it is right. So, Helms had another report prepared within two weeks that was more to the liking of Johnson and Rusk.

From that moment on it was no longer a one-shot deal intended to generate one report; spying on Americans who were working to change things became part of the CIA's job. A Special Operations Group had been formed to prepare the first report. In the summer of 1968 the program became an ongoing operation and was given the oddly appropriate code name "Operation Chaos."

Shortly after Nixon took office, Helms presented him and his secretary of state, Henry Kissinger, with a revised version of the report submitted to Johnson. The report was now given the poetic title *Restless Youth*. Helms sent a letter along with it, in which he noted the delicacy of the matter:

> In an effort to round-out our discussion of the subject, we have included a section on American students. This is an area not within the charter of this Agency, so I need not emphasize how extremely sensitive this makes the paper. Should anyone learn of its existence it would prove most embarrassing for all concerned.

Far from balking at the report and the idea of spying on Americans, Nixon supported Operation Chaos and continued to make ever greater demands on it. Although there was some disagreement over the program within the CIA itself, it continued to expand. This finally led the CIA to be involved in an interagency plan drawn up by White House aide Tom Charles Huston. The Huston Plan, as it came to be known, differed from Operation Chaos in one major respect: Coverage of the student protest and antiwar movement would no longer be limited to simply gathering intelligence. Huston outlined a plan for a direct attack on the dissidents of America. Combining the services of the CIA, the FBI and other agencies, he proposed that burglary, wiretapping and mail opening all be used to crack the protest movement wide open.

Nixon approved the plan on July 23, 1970. When his attorney general, John Mitchell, got a look at it, however, he saw how it screamed of illegality and had Nixon back off from it. Helms played along the whole way—as DCI he felt bound to serve the president—but ultimately the plan came to nothing. That didn't mean that all action against those considered to be enemies was stopped.

WATERGATE

At 2:00 A.M. on Saturday, June 17, 1972, five men were caught trying to install eavesdropping devices at the

Democratic National Committee headquarters at the Watergate Hotel in Washington. Sometime later Saturday evening, Helms received a call informing him of the break-in. He wasn't just being kept up to date on current events. One of the five burglars, James McCord, was a former high-level officer of the CIA, and another, Eugenio Martinez, was a CIA contract employee, a veteran of Operation Mongoose. Martinez was still being paid a modest sum by the agency in order to retain his services. Furthermore, notebooks found on two of the other burglars contained the name of a former CIA station chief and Bay of Pigs veteran E. Howard Hunt.

Hunt's name was perhaps the most troubling. Helms had known Hunt for years. Hunt had rather idolized Helms, in part because he saw him as the ultimate intelligence professional, and also because Helms always seemed to be bailing him out of trouble. When Hunt had been station chief in Uruguay in the early 1960s, he got into serious trouble in an attempt to go over the head of the U.S. ambassador and lobby the president of Uruguay directly in order to be kept on at his post. Such a breach would normally get a man fired, but Helms saw to it that Hunt was merely recalled to Washington. Later, when Hunt was denied a position as deputy station chief in Spain (the ambassador he'd run afoul of in Uruguay blocked his path), Helms managed to get Hunt a posting in Spain outside of the embassy.

There were several other such instances of Helms looking out for Hunt. Why did he do it? It may be simply that he liked the spy books that Hunt wrote. Nevertheless, they were never what one would call close friends, nor truly even social aquaintances. Indeed, after Hunt took an early retirement from the agency in 1970, Helms didn't hear much of him for almost 18 months.

At one point during those 18 months, Hunt made contact with Chuck Colson, a fellow Brown University graduate, who was then well connected to the White House. Colson made Hunt a rather startling proposition—to work for the White House doing the things he used to do for the CIA, things he was very good at, such as discrediting enemies.

Hunt accepted. He was given three assignments. First, he was to ruin the memory of President John F. Kennedy and his brother Robert by making a direct connection between them and the murder of Diem. (Nixon wanted to demoralize liberals in America by making the Kennedys look bad.) He was also asked to ruin their surviving brother, Senator Edward Kennedy, with further revelations about the scandal of Chappaquiddick (a woman in a car Kennedy was driving died when Kennedy drove the car off a bridge into a pond). He was also to ruin Daniel Ellsberg, the man who leaked the Pentagon Papers (a secret history of the U.S. involvement in Vietnam, written by the Pentagon) to the *New York Times.*

The first target on the agenda was Ellsberg. The idea was to create the impression that Ellsberg was unstable. Ellsberg had a psychiatrist in Los Angeles and Hunt and his team wanted a look at his files. No psychiatrist would turn over files on a patient, so they decided to burglarize his office to steal the files on Ellsberg.

Hunt would need some specialized equipment and support for operations such as these, and he knew where to get it—his old employer, the CIA. In August 1971, Colson contacted the agency and arranged for Hunt to be given the assistance he asked for, with the understanding that Hunt would be carrying out special work for the White House. Hunt arranged with the Technical Services Division (the office within Clandestine Services that makes all the spy gadgetry) for the use of a hidden camera and disguise materials. Hunt continued to ask for favors throughout August. When Hunt failed to return the materials he had borrowed supposedly for a one-time operation, the agency complained to a key Nixon aide, John Ehrlichman, at the White House, and Ehrlichman agreed to put an end to it. Hunt received no further assistance from the CIA.

Hunt and some hired hands broke into the office of Ellsberg's psychiatrist on September 3, 1971. It doesn't appear that they found what they were looking for. On another front, Ehrlichman and Nixon went directly to Helms and requested any files Helms might have on the murder of Diem and the Bay of Pigs among other things, presumably to see if there was anything that could be used to discredit the Kennedys. Although he initially hesitated, Helms did turn over the files. There is no indication that Hunt ever used them as part of his effort, nor indeed if he ever even saw them.

When the Watergate break-in occurred, Helms probably knew at once what was going on. He knew Hunt was connected to Colson, and he knew Colson was connected to the Committee to Re-elect the President (CREEP). It didn't take much to figure that somehow it would all lead to the White House. What Helms also knew, however, was that the CIA had recently been in contact with Hunt and had given him assistance. Helms did not want that to come out—he didn't want the agency to be dragged into the whole scandalous mess.

Other people wanted to do just that, however. As the FBI pursued its investigation of the break-in, they began to close in on some men in Mexico who would lead directly to CREEP. White House aide John Dean then had an idea: Why not use the CIA to block the FBI's investigation? Everyone liked the idea and Nixon's chief of staff, H.R. Haldeman, took the request to Helms.

Although initially reluctant, Helms did note that there was a long-standing agreement between the CIA and the FBI that they would refrain from exposing each other's *assets*—agents. Using this agreement, Helms did get the FBI to back off. But, when Dean tried to press his luck and get Helms to pay the bribe money that the arrested burglars were requesting to keep quiet, Helms balked. He would not allow the agency to be used to run the cover-up.

There was a time, in mid-September 1972, while he was running for reelection, that Nixon figured he had the whole Watergate deal sewn up—all the leaks were plugged and all the loose ends were tied up. The burglars had been indicted and there was no mention of the connection to CREEP. Feeling safe, Nixon's response was to go headhunting. He reportedly told Dean and Haldeman, "I want the most comprehensive notes on all those who tried to do us in. They didn't have to do it . . . they were doing this quite deliberately and they are asking for it and they are going to get it."

After his landslide reelection in November, Nixon decided to clean house. All White House aides were asked to tender resignations, as were all cabinet members; not all resignations would be accepted, but Nixon wanted that option. Helms thought that the job of DCI, not traditionally a political appointment, would not be included in the sweeping overhaul. When he was summoned to meet with Nixon at Camp David on November 20, he assumed it was on some other matter. Helms was wrong. He had been summoned to be fired.

Helms was out; his 30-year career in intelligence was over—and he knew why: Watergate. It was because he hadn't gone the extra yard for Nixon earlier in the year when Dean started setting up the agency to run the cover-up.

As a sort of consolation prize, Nixon offered him an ambassadorship of his choice. Helms chose Iran. Some have suggested that Helms blackmailed Nixon into awarding him this post, threatening to tell all he knew about the break-in and the cover-up if he didn't get the job. That seems unlikely. Nixon probably gave Helms the post either because he felt some small amount of guilt for ousting him, or because he was afraid of Helms and what he knew, and he hoped that this would keep him satisfied and quiet.

As destructive as Watergate was for Helms—it cost him his job—at least it was played out in private. For a man devoted to anonymity, the true horror of the final insult that was to come was that it was very much in the public eye.

HELMS AND THE LAW

The trouble began for Helms several months after he'd left Langley. He was in a holding pattern before he could assume the ambassadorship in Iran. Muckraking *Washington Post* columnist Jack Anderson had uncovered some evidence of ITT's involvement in the attempt to keep Allende from being elected in Chile. Anderson's columns prompted an inquiry by a subcommittee of the Senate Foreign Relations Committee, the same group that also confirms or denies a president's designate for ambassador. On February 5, 1973, Helms appeared before the committee. Because the subject of ITT and Chile was in the air, a few of the questions he was asked drifted into dangerous territory. Fortunately for Helms, the questions were phrased in such a way—was "the CIA using ITT for purposes of espionage"—that he could categorically deny the CIA's involvement without lying. Helms had dodged a bullet—a bullet that the committee didn't even know it had fired.

Helms wasn't so lucky a few days later. Everything had gone fine with his public confirmation hearing so far as the committee was concerned, but they did have a few more questions to ask—niggling issues about Watergate and whether or not the CIA had been training local police forces. So Helms was called back to testify before the executive on February 7. Helms was being queried by Senator Stuart Symington—someone Helms thought of as a friend—on a variety of things, when Symington asked a series of questions out of the blue:

> Senator Symington: Did you try in the Central Intelligence Agency to overthrow the government of Chile?
> Mr. Helms: No sir.
> Senator Symington: Did you have money passed to the opponents of Allende?
> Mr. Helms: No, sir.
> Senator Symington: So the stories you were involved in that war are wrong?
> Mr. Helms: Yes, sir. I said to Senator Fulbright many months ago that if the Agency had really gotten behind the other candidates and spent a lot of money and so forth the election might have come out differently.

But of course the CIA *had* been involved in plans to overthrow Allende after he was elected, the agency *did* pass money to his opponents, and the stories that the CIA was involved in that coup *weren't* wrong. One can understand why Helms responded as he did: He didn't want to open up that whole can of worms. If he had tried to be more honest and answered, "Well, not exactly . . ." the entire affair would have blown up in his face. Nevertheless, Helms was under oath when he appeared before the senators, and later, U.S. prosecutors would say that his responses constituted perjury.

Helms's testimony went unchallenged for three years. Then, concrete evidence turned up showing that the United States had in fact tried to keep Allende from office. In reviewing Helms's testimony before the Senate Foreign Relations Committee, the exchange between Helms and Symington was discovered.

This was the election year of 1976. The inquiry began to focus on Helms while President Gerald Ford was still in office. The inquiry got so hot that Helms decided to quit his post. On the day Jimmy Carter was elected, Ford announced that Helms would be stepping down as ambassador to Iran.

The effort to prosecute Helms for perjury would now be carried out under the Carter administration. But there was no Democrats versus Republicans politics at work here—Carter had no wish to try Helms; indeed Attorney General Griffin Bell later said that it was one of the toughest cases to come before him. But, in this post-Watergate era, no one could afford to appear soft on misconduct by officials: Perjury is perjury, whether you're a DCI or a bricklayer. Sometime around the middle of January 1977, before Carter's inauguration, Helms was officially informed that he was the subject of a grand jury investigation.

For a time, Helms was intent on contesting the charges. His defense would have been that the CIA had never *directly* funded Alessandri (the money had gone through middlemen). He also would have stated that the CIA never attempted to overthrow Allende, just prevent him from being confirmed after he'd won the election. It's questionable whether or not any judge or jury would have bought such fine distinctions. On the other hand, Helms did not want to go to trial; he wanted to clear his name, but he didn't want agency business dragged out into the open.

In the end, he didn't have to. With the backing of President Carter, Attorney General Bell approached Helms's lawyer,

Edward Bennett Williams. The attorney general offered a deal that would, in exchange for a plea of guilty, drop the charges against Helms to a misdemeanor. They negotiated for months; Helms wanted certain words deleted from the charge and wanted to make sure it wouldn't affect his pension. Finally the deal was hammered out. Unfortunately for them, they ended up with a judge who wasn't entirely keen on the deal. After giving Helms a tongue-lashing—"You now stand before this court in disgrace and shame"—he passed sentence: a $2,000 fine (the maximum) and a two-year suspended sentence.

Talking to reporters outside, Helms's laywer, Williams, said that his client should "wear this conviction like a badge of honor." Helms concurred, saying that he didn't "feel disgraced at all. I think if I had done anything else I would have been disgraced."

In his biography of Helms, Thomas Powers writes:

> After talking with reporters outside the courthouse for a few moments Helms drove off to Bethesda, Maryland, where he dropped in at a luncheon of four hundred retired CIA officers at the Kenwood Country Club. There he was greeted by a standing ovation. Two wastebaskets were put up on a piano and filled with cash and personal checks donated to pay Helms's $2,000 fine. The following day, Richard Helms's picture appeared on the front pages of newspapers for what would probably be the last time.

And for that, one imagines, Helms must have been glad.

8

THE DISMANTLING OF THE CIA: SCHLESINGER TO TURNER

With Helms out of the DCI office in Langley, Nixon was given another chance to put his stamp on the CIA. He distrusted the career professionals, the ones who, it seemed, had been in the agency since they were out of diapers. So Nixon turned to the outside. To be Helms's successor, he chose someone who had drafted a report on the state of the intelligence community for Kissinger. The man was James Schlesinger.

Schlesinger's 1971 report, *A Review of the Intelligence Community*, didn't mince words: The DCI was supposed to be the head of the intelligence community, but he wasn't by a long shot; the cost of the intelligence community was easily twice what Congress thought it was; the CIA was hopelessly insular. When Schlesinger walked into the job of DCI two years later, in January 1973, his opinions had not changed. He is reported to have said, "This is a gentleman's club, and I am no gentleman."

Schlesinger didn't like the fact that so many of the people at the top in the agency had all gone to the same elite colleges and had been at the CIA together for so long. And for him, the

James Schlesinger, the DCI who succeeded Richard Helms, and whose brief tenure was marked by a dismissal of hundreds of CIA officers. [Credit: UPI/Bettmann Newsphotos]

part of the agency that most exemplified this aspect was the Directorate of Plans, Clandestine Services, heavily staffed as it was with old OSS hands.

Early on, Schlesinger met with several hundred of the Clandestine Services officers in the CIA's auditorium. No one really knew why they were there. He talked about this and that—how he wanted more emphasis on technical intelligence gathering, less on secret agents. People still didn't know why they were there. But then he said something about new blood, and some started to realize what he was really getting at: heads were going to roll.

Schlesinger, with Nixon's full support and encouragement, wanted to haul the deadwood out of the agency. This he did, and by all accounts it was ruthless. People were fired often simply on the basis of how long they had been with the agency—over 20 years and they were out. Schlesinger was so hated that he was assigned extra bodyguards, and a video camera was aimed at his portrait in a CIA hallway to make sure that no one defaced it.

Schlesinger was only DCI for a very short time—five months, the shortest tenure of all the DCIs so far. But in that brief span he fired nearly 1,400 officers. He was essentially brought in as a hatchet man, and when the job was done, he was transferred to the Defense Department.

Schlesinger's replacement as DCI was an inside man, one of the few remaining old OSS hands—William Colby. It is hard to imagine morale at the agency being any lower than it was when Schlesinger began the mass firings, but it would sink even lower under Colby. If Schlesinger was hated, it was at least acknowledged that he was someone brought in from the outside to do the president's bidding. Colby, however, was an insider, and for his blows against the agency he was considered a traitor.

Helms had taken Colby under his wing. They were both OSS veterans, and while Colby was a Princeton graduate, he, like Helms, was not a part of the elite college clubbiness. And yet they differed in their views of intelligence. Helms believed in the importance of human spies, while Colby was more of a Bissell type—he liked a mix of technical spying and covert operations. Despite these differences, however, it seems that Helms was somehow involved in almost every major promotion Colby received. This is what made Colby's betrayal, as Helms saw it, all the more painful.

The trouble that eventually rocked the CIA began while Schlesinger was still DCI. In early 1973, not long after Helms had left Langley, the E. Howard Hunt trail led Watergate investigators to the discovery of the "Plumbers." As was subsequently found out, the Plumbers, Hunt et al., were assigned by the White House to do more than simply "fix leaks." The most notorious operation, next to the Watergate break-in, was the burglary of Daniel Ellsberg's psychiatrist's office. The worst part of all of this, so far as the CIA was concerned, was that the agency was connected to the Ellsberg operation. In August 1971, on White House orders, the agency's Technical Services Division had supplied Hunt with some of the spy equipment he later used in the burglary. This was the secret that Helms had worked so hard to keep from coming out. Out it came.

Schlesinger was outraged. He was not so terribly angry just because the CIA was linked to Hunt, but because he hadn't been told of it.

By this time, Colby had managed to work his way into Schlesinger's good graces. To an extent, Colby had become Schlesinger's guide in the agency, his inside man and ally. Colby was promoted by Schlesinger to head of Clandestine Services (which underwent yet another name change under Schlesinger, from Directorate of Plans back to Directorate of Operations). Schlesinger knew that his plans to revamp the agency would find the most resistance in Clandestine Services; it was Colby's job to take care of that for him. Colby wasn't keen on being a hatchet man, but he followed orders and met his quota of firings. If that was the hardship of heading up Clandestine Services, the reward was his close relationship with the DCI and the strong possibility that he was in the right position to succeed him.

As perhaps Schlesinger's closest advisor in the agency, Colby came up with a radical idea for dealing with the flap over Hunt and the Plumbers. He proposed that officers throughout the agency be encouraged to report on anything that had been undertaken at the CIA and they considered to be questionable. This way, if they could find out exactly what skeletons were hanging in what closets, there would be no further surprises for Schlesinger or any other succeeding DCI.

Schlesinger thought it was a good plan and gave his approval. A memo was circulated on the subject, telling agency officers to reveal any potential embarrassments they might know of. But, as it happened, by that time Schlesinger already had one foot out the door on his way to the Department of Defense, and Colby was set to replace him.

Skeletons marched out of closets in great numbers over the next few months. After all the soul baring was done, the result was a 693-page report that received the nickname the "Family Jewels." It was all there—the assassination plots, the mind-altering drug tests on unsuspecting citizens, the Chilean election meddling, the domestic spying. But that was as far as it was supposed to go. Colby had intended it not only as a way to prevent further embarrassing surprises, but also as a form of catharsis, of bloodletting. People had the chance to get these secrets off their chests. But, it was all supposed to happen behind closed doors. It was all to remain secret.

However laudable Colby's motives may or may not have been, to Helms and other intelligence observers he had broken two cardinal rules of intelligence by compiling the Family Jewels. Rule number one is one of the bedrock principles of the CIA: Everything works on a need-to-know basis. That is, all information is compartmentalized. Colby broke this rule by putting together all this information *in one place.* And he broke another major rule by actually having a report—a 693-page report at that—written up. The rule he broke: *Never put anything in writing.*

The summer of 1974 was a frenzied one for Washington and the country at large. The growing evidence of White House involvement in the attempt to cover up the Watergate break-in resulted in a first in American history: the resignation of a president. Nixon left office in August 1974 and Vice President Gerald Ford took the office of president.

It was sometime later that year, in the fall, that reporter Seymour Hersh of the *New York Times* pieced together the parts of the puzzle. Once together, they seemed to indicate that the CIA had been involved in a domestic spying operation. Hersh had uncovered Operation Chaos, although he didn't yet know that was the program's name. He went to talk to Colby about it on December 20, 1974. Colby could honestly deny certain allegations, for he had put an end to the remaining traces of Chaos—the mail opening, in particular—shortly after he became DCI. Hersh's other questions posed problems, though. Instead of lying, Colby tried to explain, stating that the targets had all been foreign nationals—the contacts of American protestors, not the protestors themselves. But those were qualifications, not denials. Colby had in effect admitted that the CIA had been involved in domestic spying.

Hersh's story came out two days later and there was an immediate public outcry. In response, President Ford assigned Vice President Nelson Rockefeller to head a commission of inquiry into the accusations of domestic spying. Ford had also seen all he needed to see of the Family Jewels to know what secrets the CIA was trying to hide. The Rockefeller Commission was in some ways an effort to forestall further investigation. The commission was stacked with conservatives and was to confine itself to the issue of domestic spying. They weren't going to get into the assassination plots and other dark corners.

It was actually Ford himself who leaked the most damaging information, at a lunch with the publisher and managing editor of the *New York Times*. He said the Rockefeller Commission had been stacked with conservatives because, otherwise, it might probe too deeply into the CIA and uncover the really bad stuff—like assassinations. After blurting this out, he realized his gaffe and insisted he was speaking off the record. The *Times* reluctantly agreed to hold off on the story, but word of what Ford had said leaked out.

Daniel Schorr, a reporter for CBS, tried to track the story down, but he couldn't find anything to support the supposed assassinations. He was about to give up until he asked Colby a simple question. Schorr had been working under the misapprehension that the assassinations had taken place in the United States and asked Colby if such things had happened. Colby again made a mistake. Instead of denying it outright—which would have been the truth, because there had been no plans to assassinate anyone in America—he answered, "Not in this country." Colby's response clearly implied that the CIA had carried out assassinations in other countries.

The public outcry that followed the earlier accusations of domestic spying was nothing compared to the outrage that came on the heels of Schorr's subsequent story on the CBS news. Senator Frank Church quickly headed up a committee to look into the alleged CIA wrongdoings. Over the course of his investigation, which ended with the submission of a report

James Jesus Angleton, the CIA's onetime chief of counterespionage, the most complex and convoluted part of the spy business. Angleton is shown here after appearing before President Ford's Rockefeller Commission inquiry into alleged CIA wrongdoings. For Angleton, whose life had been devoted to the agency, the public exposure of the CIA must have been tremendously painful. [Credit: UPI/ Bettmann Newsphotos]

on November 20, 1975, every little bit of the CIA's Family Jewels was exposed to the light of day.

According to Helms and others, their problem with Colby was not that he told all to the Church Committee, but that he told them "more than all." Helms had to testify, as did many others at the CIA, past and present. Nothing came out that went beyond what was included in the Family Jewels. The final conclusion of the committee on the subject of assassinations was that while they had been planned, they had never been carried out.

It was during the Church Committee investigation that morale at the CIA reached its low point (although, ironically, when the stories of assassination plots and general cloak and dagger skullduggery came to light in this period, applications to join the CIA tripled). Colby's rationale for cooperating was the hope that by volunteering the dark secrets, he could safely protect the really important secrets. At all costs, he wanted to avoid exposing agents' names, intelligence-gathering methods and so on.

This didn't wash with Helms and others. One of those was James Angleton, the head of counterintelligence. For a variety of reasons, Angleton and Colby did not like each other. Basically, Angleton accused Colby of being sloppy when it came to counterintelligence. He felt, in particular, that Colby had blood on his hands from his days in Vietnam when he had

Former DCI Richard Helms (left) and then-current DCI William Colby (seated next to him) appear before the Senate Armed Services Committee. Helms felt personally betrayed by Colby, his onetime protégé, when Colby instigated an investigation into a possible charge of perjury against Helms for his testimony regarding the CIA's involvement in the Chilean elections. Helms also felt Colby betrayed the agency as a whole by revealing so many of its secrets. [Credit: UPI/ Bettmann Newsphotos]

failed to detect the 40,000 agents of the North that had infiltrated the South.

For his part, Colby thought Angleton's suspicion had reached absurd levels. There may have been other personal differences involved as well. The professional tension was so strong between the two men that Colby tried to persuade Schlesinger to fire Angleton. He failed. But when Colby became DCI he did manage to get Angleton out, and with him went much of the agency's counterintelligence capabilities.

When Angleton saw what was happening during the Church Committee investigations, he reportedly remarked that he didn't see how Colby could have wreaked as much harm if he had been working for the enemy. Others went further, saying they seriously thought Colby might indeed be a Soviet agent, perhaps recruited by the Russians when he was working in Rome in the 1950s. There has never been anything even remotely supporting such a charge.

Helms's reason for being upset with Colby actually had nothing to do with the Church Committee. Colby had been informed in 1973 that there might be some discrepancy between what Helms had said to the Senate Foreign Relations Committee about the CIA's involvement in Chile and what had actually happened. Colby appointed a three-man group to look into this. In the report, one of the men went further than "discrepancy": He said Helms had committed perjury. Colby sat on the report for some time. Then, in 1974, fearing what would happen if it ever became public that he had known of the matter and done nothing about it, he passed the report on to the Justice Department. This eventually led to Helms being charged.

Colby was at the helm of the agency during its roughest years. Fittingly, in a way, not long after things calmed down, he left. He stepped down as DCI on January 30, 1976, a few months after the submission of the Church Committee report. In Colby's place, President Ford appointed fellow Republican George Bush.

Bush ran the agency for a little over a year. His tenure was free of the intense scrutiny that had hounded the agency for the previous several years. In many ways the CIA was in a holding pattern—it didn't move one way or the other, almost like an accident victim who is told to lie still. One major accomplishment under Bush was the December 1976 launch of the first KH-11 spy satellite. This satellite was the first to be able to provide near "real time" images. With previous satellites there could be a lag time of days, even weeks, before the pictures taken could be looked at. With the KH-11, pictures could be viewed within a matter of hours. Bush left in March 1977. He was replaced by Admiral Stansfield Turner, an appointee of newly elected President Jimmy Carter.

Turner had two strikes against him going into the job of DCI: He was an "outsider," and the agency was virtually at the lowest ebb in its history. As a four-star admiral with remarkable intelligence (he'd been a Rhodes scholar), however, Turner was respected and did manage to set the CIA on a defined course. The course was defined, in part, by the election of Jimmy Carter, who had campaigned on the promise of bringing ethics back to Washington. Under Turner, the emphasis at the CIA would be on intelligence gathering and analysis. Covert activity would be reduced to a bare minimum.

The accomplishments of the agency in the Turner years were not tampered elections or secret wars but the cultivation of new intelligence sources, both human and technical. One great technical advance involved tapping into Soviet underwater communications cables. Another was Indigo, a spy satellite program that researched the possibility of radar imaging satellites (satellites that can take pictures with radar can do so through cloud cover, which had always been the bane of earlier spy satellites). Turner's CIA also recruited a member of the Polish general staff, Colonel Kuklinski, and developed a couple of *assets* (Soviets recruited to spy for the United States) within the Soviet Union.

But the reason for steering away from covert operations was not just because of Carter's philosophy. After the horrendous upheaval of the Church Committee investigations, the officers in Clandestine Services were markedly gun-shy. Turner had tried, quietly, to sound out Clandestine Services

President Jimmy Carter at Camp David with his top military and intelligence advisors to discuss the developments in Iran. Left to right: DCI Stansfield Turner, Secretary of Defense Harold Brown, Chairman of the Joint Chiefs of Staff General David Jones, Vice President Walter Mondale, National Security Advisor Zbigniew Brzezinski, President Carter and Secretary of State Cyrus Vance. [Credit: UPI/Bettmann Newsphotos]

on what they thought of backing a moderate leader in Guatemala and building him up to eventually take power. They didn't want to get involved. Turner also queried agents on what could be done to remove the three thorns in America's side—Qaddafi in Libya, Castro in Cuba and the Ayatollah Khomeini in Iran. Clandestine Services didn't want to touch that with a 10-foot pole. President Ford had signed an executive order banning assassinations and Carter had reaffirmed it when he took office: The agents didn't even want to talk about it.

It was the last thorn mentioned, Khomeini, who caused Turner the most trouble and, in effect, cost Carter the presidency. The CIA was well wired into Iran, but they did not predict the fall of the Shah. This intelligence catastrophe was later blamed on the CIA being tied too closely to the Shah's secret police, the Savak. The feeling was that the CIA had relied so heavily on the Savak that it had become complacent and isolated from what was happening "out in the streets." CIA analysts did not think that the religious fervor sweeping Iran would become *that* important. They never considered that an aging religious leader, exiled in Paris, would return to take over the country. When in a wave of anti-American fervor (because the United States had supported the shah) hostages were seized at the embassy in Teheran, it became apparent that the agency had failed to predict many very important outcomes.

The CIA would play a part in planning a rescue attempt, using the KH-11 spy satellite to map assault and escape routes. Unfortunately, the attempt came to a fiery end in the Iranian desert when two commando helicopters crashed.

Like Carter's presidency, Turner's tenure as DCI would never recover from the scandal of the Iran affair. It wasn't long after the November election of Ronald Reagan that Turner realized his days at Langley were probably numbered. Indeed, there were signs throughout the campaign that he might not be kept on. Reagan had vowed to rebuild America's intelligence capacity, to get it moving again, and to most observers it didn't look like Turner would be part of that rebuilding. There was great rejoicing at the CIA when Reagan was elected. The only misgivings were in Turner's office. The misgivings turned out to be justified. On January 28, 1981, eight days after Reagan was inaugurated, a new DCI was sworn in—ex-OSS officer and Reagan campaign manager William Casey.

9

THE CASEY YEARS

To intelligence observers, William Casey was not the obvious choice to be the new DCI. That honor fell to Admiral Bobby Ray Inman, a man with 30 years of experience in the intelligence community. Most notable was his stint as the head of the National Security Agency. Although Inman wasn't in the CIA, Reagan and his team wanted someone who was even more of an outsider. They wanted Inman on board but only as deputy director, a posting Inman initially refused but finally accepted. He lasted a little over two years. He and Casey had never seen eye to eye and, after 30 years of service to his country and little in the way of financial security to show for it, he decided it was time to work for himself.

For Reagan and his advisors, Casey had the perfect inside/outside credentials. At the end of World War II he'd been running several teams of agents in Germany for the OSS. Casey's mentor, and something of a father figure to him as well, was "Wild Bill" Donovan. There were still a number of OSS veterans in the CIA—not all had been purged by Schlesinger, and Casey's war record would help him manage the agency. Yet, Casey was not an intelligence careerist. Part of the problem with "insiders," according to observers in Reagan's camp, is that they sometimes show more loyalty to the agency than to the president they are supposed to serve. This would not be a problem with Casey. He hadn't spent the previous 30 years in intelligence; he'd spent it amassing a tidy fortune in speculative business. And, as Reagan's campaign manager, he wouldn't have to be brought on board. He was already part of the team and was, of course, suitably conservative enough to tow the new ideological line.

Casey's views on intelligence were consistent with those Reagan had been espousing during the campaign. The feeling was that the CIA had become a mere shadow of its former self; it had become weak and ineffective. Reagan vowed to rebuild, and Casey was eager to do it for him. What they meant by all of this talk of rebuilding was that they wanted to revitalize Clandestine Services and start running covert operations again.

The only real problem with Casey becoming DCI was that it wasn't exactly what he had wanted. He had really hoped that he would be named as secretary of state. When Alexander Haig got that job, Casey felt in a sense he had to settle for leading the CIA. The DCI was not traditionally part of the Cabinet, not part of the policy-forming inner circle. This was what Casey had wanted, to be part of the decision-making process, to be one of the pilots charting the course. If he couldn't be secretary of state, formulating the nation's overt foreign policy, then Casey figured he could elevate the position of DCI to near Cabinet status by running the nation's covert foreign policy.

Casey's appearance as a sort of "shadow secretary of state" was one thing that characterized his tenure as DCI. The other distinguishing characteristic was his enthusiasm for covert operations. He felt that the CIA, of all institutions, shouldn't be afraid to take risks: If the job was worth doing, he was willing to take the flack.

There is a rumor about Casey that illustrates his "let's do it" approach. At one point it was decided that it would be a good idea to get a listening device into the office of a high-ranking official in the Middle East. But the agents at Clandestine

Services hemmed and hawed over how to get the bug in place; they didn't know how they could get an agent into the office without risking his capture. Casey was reportedly annoyed by the inaction, so he embarked on a tour of the Middle East, visited the office of this high-ranking official, and put the bug in place himself (according to various versions of the story, it was either concealed in the spine of a book he presented as a gift, or it was hidden in a pin he plunged into a seat cushion).

Casey's tenure saw further improvements in spy satellite technology, and one major setback in that arena—the explosion of the space shuttle *Challenger*. That January 1986 disaster, which took the lives of seven astronauts, shut down the shuttle program for almost three years, eliminating the only way of getting reconnaissance satellites into space.

This caused something of a panic, as the last spy satellite to go up, a KH-11, went up in 1984, and that satellite had only a two-year life span. Because of the importance of these satellites, the bulk of the first slate of missions scheduled after the resumption of shuttle flights were reserved for the military.

Like virtually every DCI before him, Casey was frustrated by the agency's inability to set up agents behind the Iron Curtain. He, however, was probably a little more successful than many of the former DCIs had been. Within three years of Casey's becoming DCI, the CIA had recruited 25 new agents in the Soviet Union, other Eastern bloc nations and China. These agents ranged from highly placed government officials to physicists to agents of enemy intelligence services.

But satellites and agents-in-place were not the primary concerns of the CIA under Casey. There were four things that obsessed Casey, indeed the entire Reagan administration: international terrorism, Libya, Nicaragua and Iran.

TERRORISM

Fighting terrorists is like fighting an ever moving guerilla war. The enemy poses a shadowy figure, able to blend into the population, never easy to identify, almost impossible to catch and prosecute. Terrorism, as is one of its intents, creates a lot of helpless rage, especially in a country such as the United States, which prides itself on its military muscle. Casey surely felt this frustration. There were efforts throughout Casey's tenure to infiltrate and undermine terrorist organizations.

However, it was in the wake of the October 1983 bombing of the U.S. Marine Corps barracks in Beirut, which claimed the lives of more than 200 Marines, that efforts to curb terrorism really stepped into high gear. Two stories illustrate the two different approaches that the U.S. intelligence community took to fight terrorism.

After Reagan's reelection in 1984, Casey looked for a way to fight directly against the terrorists. He had a certain amount of admiration for the way the Soviets handled such matters. When Soviet diplomats were kidnapped in Beirut by the Party of God, an extremist, fundamentalist Moslem terrorist group, the KGB in turn kidnapped a member of the Party of God. They killed him in a brutal way and sent the body back to the Party of God. The Soviet diplomats were released soon after.

Casey's idea was to set up hit squads in the Mideast. Closely informed by agents infiltrating the various terrorist groups, the hit squads were supposed to head off terrorist attacks, or, presumably if that failed, hit back in response. Casey didn't want the CIA to use its own agents in these hit squads; he wanted them to be made up of Lebanese. Training the Lebanese in this capacity, however, didn't work, and the CIA eventually backed out of the operation.

That didn't mean that covert plans to counter terrorism stopped, however. Casey arranged with the Saudi Arabians through a middle man, Saudi Prince Bandar, to carry out a reprisal on Sheikh Fadlallah. The sheikh was the head of the Party of God (the same group that had the run-in with the Soviets). He was responsible for a number of anti-American terrorist acts in the region. The plan was simple: Blow Fadlallah up. A huge bomb was detonated outside Fadlallah's apartment building. Although 80 people were killed, Fadlallah miraculously emerged unscathed. Frustrated, the Saudis tried a different approach. They went to Fadlallah and offered him $2 million if he would halt all anti-U.S. attacks.

He accepted, and since then there have been no more Party of God-sponsored actions against America. As Prince Bandar noted, "It was easier to bribe him than to kill him."

Another antiterrorist response went much more smoothly, did not cause any loss of life and was undoubtedly one of the intelligence coups of the decade. In October 1985, a group of terrorists hijacked a Mediterranean cruise ship, the *Achille Lauro*. The ship had Americans on board and one of them, Leon Klinghoffer, was killed. The terrorists then docked the ship in Egypt. This put Egyptian President Mubarak in a delicate situation: He wanted to offend neither the United States nor his Arab-world allies. So, he expelled the four terrorists from his country without prosecuting them.

What the CIA knew, however, was that even though Mubarak said the terrorists had left Egypt, they were still actually there. The National Security Agency had intercepted Mubarak's communications. They knew where the terrorists were being held and on what flight they were being flown out of Egypt. The Defense Department was notified. In a rather daring move, the plane flying the terrorists out of Egypt was intercepted by U.S. fighters over the Mediterranean and forced to land in Sicily. The Italians were willing to prosecute the terrorists.

But actions against this terrorist group or that one were not what Casey and the Reagan administration really wanted. They wanted to go after the country where a lot of the terrorists were being trained; they wanted to stop the man they knew was funding much of the region's terrorist activity. They were really after Libya and its leader, Muammar Qaddafi.

LIBYA

Libya had been a major target of U.S. intelligence gathering activities for years for one major reason: This oil-rich nation was using its billions to buy huge amounts of weaponry from the Soviets. Libya was by no means a puppet of the Soviets—unlike Cuba, it wasn't being *given* the weapons; still, the relationship seemed far too friendly for the liking of the

Leader of Libya, Colonel Moammar Qaddafi (in uniform, with swagger stick), with Soviet leader Leonid Brezhnev (in black hat) at the Moscow airport during Qaddafi's 1981 visit to the Soviet Union. Although Qaddafi does have ties to the Soviet Union—he buys billions of dollars of military equipment from them—what concerns the United States more is his open sponsorship of terrorism. [Credit: UPI/Bettmann Newsphotos]

United States. The United States was also concerned about Libya because of Qaddafi.

If Qaddafi seemed flamboyant, perhaps even a little clownish at times, he was also very much in control of his nation. Even worse, he was also unpredictable, and that was worrisome—no one wanted a rogue friend of the Soviets on the loose in North Africa. But what really damned Qaddafi in the eyes of the Americans was evidence showing Libya as a booster of terrorism in the region in the late 1970s. There were, then, many reasons for wanting to get Qaddafi out of power.

The first major covert operation under Casey was perhaps the most successful such operation under his tenure. CIA analysts discovered that Qaddafi's weakest point was his involvement in the civil war in Chad, the country to the south of Libya. They also discovered that Qaddafi had many foes beyond the United States: Egypt, France, the Sudan and others were all annoyed and perhaps a little afraid of him, and these countries were backing the opposition in the Chad war. So, the CIA jumped on the secret bandwagon, and with the approval of President Reagan, the agency channeled funds to ex-Chad Defense Minister Hissein Habre.

Although some later questioned whether or not Habre was the best man to support—his name was associated with massacres and he had at one time espoused his admiration for the likes of Mao and Ho Chi Minh—the support did eventually pay off. In June 1982, Habre entered the Chadian capital of N'Djamena and took control. Qaddafi's southern expansion had been stopped.

But the question that Casey wanted answered was not how to stop Qaddafi's expansion, but how to stop him—period. This question became even more important when the CIA began to get wind that Qaddafi was sending out hit squads to attack the United States at home and abroad. In the summer of 1981, a high-ranking Ethiopian official reported that at a meeting between Qaddafi and the leader of Ethiopia, Qaddafi announced that he was going to kill Reagan.

The CIA went on alert. Over the next few months reports indicated that this was no idle threat; teams had been put together and mobilized. It was even reported that a team of assassins had entered the United States through Canada and were bent on killing top U.S. officials. Although there were, thankfully, no assassination attempts, the tension between the two countries continued to grow.

As it had when dealing with other unfriendly regimes in the past, the CIA sought out Libyan dissidents to support them. When no organized resistance could be found within Libya, the agency turned to dissidents who had fled the country. There were many of these; indeed, Qaddafi was so perturbed by dissidents abroad that he dispatched hit teams to shut them up. The CIA decided to support an anti-Qaddafi group that was in exile in Egypt. The group was headed by an ex-Libyan government official, Dr. Mohammed Youssef Magarieff. Magarieff also had the tacit support of his hosts and Sudanese President Nimeiry. There was talk of military intervention and orchestration of coups and the like, but ultimately this kind of operation—building a creditable and formidable opposition—can only proceed slowly. This was especially true in the case of Libya, for as much as Qaddafi had annoyed his Arab neighbors, and as much as they wanted him gone, he was still a fellow Arab. This meant that the CIA had to move quietly and secretly or risk alienating their other Arab allies and, in the process, perhaps turn Qaddafi into a martyr.

The other path the CIA pursued was to obtain concrete evidence linking Libya to a specific terrorist act through its network of spies. The CIA knew and could prove that Libya had hosted and trained assorted terrorists; the agency even knew where the terrorist training bases were located. But they had not yet been able to say Libya was responsible for a specific bombing or hijacking. In the spring of 1986, the connection was made.

Qaddafi claims much more of the Mediterranean to be under his country's domain than international law recognizes. In particular, he has drawn an imaginary line across the mouth of the Gulf of Sidra and claims all the territory within it for Libya. He named this imaginary line *The Line of Death*. On August 19, 1981, two U.S. Navy fighters on patrol in the Gulf of Sidra were fired upon by Libyan jets. The American planes returned fire and shot down two Libyan fighters. It was only a few days later that Qaddafi first announced his intentions to have Reagan killed.

From then on, the Gulf of Sidra remained a potential flashpoint. In March 1986, in order to contest Qaddafi's claim of rule over the waters (and undoubtedly to provoke him), the United States engaged in a military maneuver code-named "Operation Prairie Fire." On March 23, U.S. Navy boats and planes crossed the Line of Death. Libya responded by attacking American planes, and the United States counterattacked by sinking two Libyan patrol boats and by launching precision HARM missiles that knocked out Libyan coastal radar stations.

Qaddafi was not pleased. On March 25, the NSA intercepted a message Libya had sent to eight of its *people's bureaus* (its name for embassies), calling on its people abroad to stand by and be ready to attack American targets. On April 4, the Libyan people's bureau of East Berlin sent a message home saying, "Tripoli will be happy when you see the headlines tomorrow." A few hours later there was another message reporting that the unnamed action was "happening now." Ten minutes later, at 1:49 A.M. Berlin time, a bomb went off in a West Berlin disco. It injured 250 people and killed one American, Sergeant Kenneth Ford, and a Turkish woman.

This information, this direct connection between Libya and a terrorist act, was used as the excuse for the American bombing of Libya on Monday, April 14, 1986. Although various industrial and military installations were targeted, one of the key targets was Qaddafi's headquarters. He, however, survived the attack.

The interception of the messages between Tripoli and its embassies was an unabashed intelligence triumph. Many within the community argued against making the exact intercepts public. They would have preferred an ambiguous description, such as "incontrovertible intelligence information," for one rule of intelligence is that as soon as you let the other side know exactly what you know, they'll be sure to figure out how you know it and will cut off your intelligence source. The Reagan administration, however, needed to be able to prove publicly that it had this link and was willing to sacrifice the intelligence source for that purpose.

Whatever one feels about the morality of the bombing attack on Libya, it did accomplish two things: It undoubtedly dampened Libya's enthusiasm for engaging in or supporting terrorist acts, and it satisfied the Reagan administration's desire to "do something about Libya." It brought down the fever. At any rate, by this time the CIA was already focusing most of its time and energy elsewhere, on a country far closer to home—Nicaragua.

NICARAGUA

One of President Jimmy Carter's major undertakings had been to campaign for human rights. Critics contended that he only criticized right-wing dictatorships and not the totalitarian (as in total control) governments of the left. He would speak out against Pinochet's brutality in Chile, but not against the labor camps in Siberia where people who angered the communist party were sent. This accusation was not really true, because Carter in fact had harsh words for all oppressors of human rights. One of the impressions of Carter that conservative critics had was that he was soft on communists. They could point to Nicaragua, where Carter had refused to lend support to an old American friend, dictator Anastasio Somoza, when he was in trouble. What further angered these critics was that after Somoza fled to Florida, Carter's administration recognized the leftist Sandinista revolutionaries (called that in memory of Augusto Sandino, a rebel leader killed in 1934) as the new government of the country and even offered them aid. Indeed, during Carter's last year in office he had lobbied hard for a bill to give Nicaragua $75 million in aid.

About six months after the Sandinistas took power, Carter began to be troubled by the revolutionary government's clampdown on all opposition and its growing ties to the Soviets. Making a major swing, he authorized the CIA to spend money to support and foster the opposition within Nicaragua. The Reagan administration wanted to do more than that.

Congress had attached some strings to the $75 million in aid to Nicaragua for which Carter had lobbied. One was that the aid could be canceled if there was any evidence that the Sandinistas were lending arms or other support to rebel groups in other Central American nations or were in any other way contributing to the unrest in the region. The CIA found such evidence. They intercepted an arms shipment from the Sandinistas to the rebels of El Salvador, and the Reagan administration canceled the aid.

Administration officials wanted to go further than simply cutting off aid to the Sandinistas, they wanted to actively support the "other side." There was, unfortunately for them, no real other side at that time, at least not militarily. So, they had to create a counterforce. The man they chose to run it was an ex-Sandinista (an important propaganda point) named Eden Pastora. Pastora, given the operational name "Commander Zero," worked with a small band out of Costa Rica. Pastora was known as a vicious, unsavory character— Deputy Director Inman characterized him as a "barracuda," and many of the men who fought with him were often little more than thugs. But he was all the CIA had to work with.

Purportedly, Pastora and 500 men (who had yet to gain the name *contras*) were to harass the Sandinistas and stop the flow of arms from Nicaragua to the Salvadorian rebels. The CIA's agreement with Congress was that they were not to seek the overthrow of the Sandinista government. As it turned out, however, that initial 500-man force quickly grew to 5,500, and the object of intercepting arms shipments was soon forgotten. For one thing, Costa Rica, where Commander Zero had his base of operations, is south of Nicaragua, while El Salvador is to the north. The object, from the beginning, was to remove the Sandinistas from power.

One question that was raised in the administration was why the CIA was handling the operation. The cover had long since been blown; the public knew the CIA was supporting the contras. Why not have the American military handle it directly, going the route of sending in "advisors?" For one thing, there was the specter of Vietnam, a conflict that had begun with advisors being sent in. As well, Secretary of Defense Caspar Weinberger did not want the Pentagon to get involved, and there would be considerable problems of international law if the United States were to take such a direct role. So, the operation remained covert, even though, for all intents and purposes, it was overt. For the first time in its history, the CIA was running an open paramilitary operation. Even the time-honored doctrine of plausible denial was ignored. Casey had said that his CIA would take risks and would ignore public criticism. He had been telling the truth.

Casey maintained tight, personal control over much of the Nicaraguan operation. When he was frustrated by the contras' lack of advances, he sent word to Pastora that he and his men should expand their range, come down out of the hills and hit the cities, thereby showing they could strike anywhere. Commander Zero's response was to send a Cessna airplane with two 500-pound bombs under its wings on a mission to the civilian airport outside of the capital of Managua. The plane crashed into the airport, killing the pilot, the co-pilot and one worker on the ground. If the plane had crashed a little later than it did, it might have taken the lives of Senator Gary Hart and Senator William Cohen, who were flying in that morning on a fact-finding mission.

The CIA's involvement in Nicaragua was supposed to be limited to advice and financial and material support. On one occasion, however, Casey sent in contract employees known as UCLAs (unilateral controlled Latino assets) to do the difficult job of raiding and destroying vital Nicaraguan oil storage depots.

Casey's involvement in and commitment to the Nicaraguan operation caused some disagreement in the agency. Some old hands called it "Casey's war." They may not have been pleased with the timidity shown by Carter and Turner, but they were also not so keen on what appeared to be the near reckless doings under Casey.

Of course, supporting the contras was not Casey's job alone. Indeed, overall control of the Nicaraguan operation was given to an interagency group. One of the key members of this group was Lieutenant Colonel Oliver North, employed by the National Security Council. One plan recommended by the group, and approved by Reagan, Casey and Secretary of State George Shultz, called for the mining of Nicaragua's harbors. The idea was to use small mines that would cause damage but wouldn't destroy ships—they were to be all bark and no bite. The idea was to scare ships away from Nicaragua, or at least scare Lloyds of London, the maritime insurer, into removing coverage for any ship going into Nicaraguan harbors. This would keep the ships away. The mines were laid.

Mining the harbors turned out to be a big mistake. Instead of crippling the Nicaraguan economy, it simply drove the Nicaraguans further into the arms of the financially accommodating Soviets. It enraged allies when their ships were damaged. Finally, as mining a country's harbors is equal to a declaration of war, Nicaragua sued the United States at the World Court and won. Although the United States ignored the verdict and refused to pay the penalty, it was a major propaganda loss and cost them dearly in world opinion.

Another major gaffe came with the discovery of a CIA-written illustrated manual for the contras titled *Psychological Operations in Guerilla Warfare*. The manual outlined possible types of operations, suggesting the use of violence, even the "neutralizing"—assassination—of local officials. This stirred up a huge controversy, sparked House and Senate investigations and became part of the debate in Reagan's 1984 reelection campaign.

Funding for the contras subsequently bogged down in Congress. So, the administration sought to keep the money flowing by other means. Casey channeled money from private American citizens and from foreign countries to the contras. The other countries included Israel, Brunei (an oil-rich sultanate on the coast of Borneo) and Saudi Arabia, which paid $1 million a month for eight months to keep the contras alive. The possibility of obtaining funds from South Africa was even explored at one point.

In October 1984, Congress cut off all funding to the contras and ordered the CIA to halt all efforts to support them. For some reason, President Daniel Ortega of Nicaragua chose that moment to visit the Soviet Union to ask for $200 million. It was a slap in the face to the United States. The Saudis acted as a stopgap, giving the contras at least another $15 million until, in October 1986, the pendulum had swung back in favor of the contras, and the Congress approved sending them $100 million.

It was also in the fall of 1986, however, that reports began to surface about a scandal that would embroil the Reagan administration for the rest of its term. The scandal involved the secret funding of the contras and a country that now had confounded two presidents—Iran.

IRAN

Iran had always been a major concern of the intelligence community and the U.S. government as a whole. When the Shah was deposed and Khomeini took power, the United States lost not only an important ally but also key intelligence assets: The CIA had vital listening posts near the Iran-Soviet border. And there was, of course, always the worry that the Iranians would someday embrace the Soviets. Indeed, there was the fear that the U.S. ban on the sale of arms to Iran and the wave of antiterrorist fervor, with all its finger-pointing at Iran, was only serving to drive the Iranians closer to the Soviets. The question then was, "How do we get back into Teheran?"

In August 1985, an avenue opened up. The United States learned that there were some moderates within Iran who might be willing to talk. Iran had been locked into a brutal war with Iraq for half a decade, and it needed weapons. In particular, it wanted American TOW antitank missiles. In return for the missiles Iran would aid in obtaining the release of American hostages held in Beirut.

To some in the Reagan administration this seemed ideal. Not only would a connection be made with moderates in Teheran, but something would be done about the horrible frustration the administration felt over the hostages. Others were not so keen on the plan. Secretary of Defense Weinberger didn't trust the Iranians and didn't like selling them arms. Secretary of State Shultz felt it would completely undermine the U.S. policy of dealing with terrorists, which had always been that there would be no negotiations and no ransom would be paid. Shultz feared that if word got out that the United States had traded arms for hostages, it would

Leader of Iran, the Ayatollah Khomeini, waves from behind a giant poster of himself. [Credit: UPI/Bettmann Newsphotos]

encourage a rash of kidnappings. DCI Casey, however, was one of those who liked the idea.

The initial plan called for the Israelis to act as an intermediary. The Israelis would sell the Iranians TOW anti-tank missiles they had on hand, and the United States would in turn replenish the Israeli stockpile. Using a middleman would allow the United States some measure of plausible denial— "No, we never sold missiles to Iran"—if the plan was uncovered. Handling the deal was Iranian arms dealer Manucher Ghorbanifar, a man whose dealings define the word "shady." When the deal threatened to fall apart because of distrust between the Iranians and Israelis—the Iranians wanted to see the missiles before they paid their millions, and the Israelis wanted to be paid before they handed over the TOWs——

Ghorbanifar brought in Saudi arms merchant Adnan Khashoggi to front the money for the Israelis. The deal went through; Iran received 508 TOW missiles and, on September 15, 1985, U.S. hostage Reverend Benjamin Weir was released.

The deal making with Iran continued. In early 1986, however, it almost broke down when U.S. representatives, including Oliver North, met with middleman Ghorbanifar and supposed Iranian moderate Hasheimi Rafsanjani. The meeting did not go well. Apparently Ghorbanifar had been lying to both sides. To Rafsanjani he had promised more advanced American weaponry, and to the Americans he had promised the release of all the hostages.

Indeed, Ghorbanifar had quite a reputation for lying. On one occasion he took a lie detector test and reportedly only answered one question honestly—what his name was. Nevertheless, the CIA continued to work with him as he was all it had, and the deal went on. Weinberger and Shultz were still opposed, and Casey was still for it. He did not want to see Iran fall to the Soviets. Subsequently, another 1,000 TOWs were sent to Iran. That marked the first direct shipment from the United States.

In April 1986, the operation took a strange turn when Oliver North, who was working on supplying the contras, realized that the profit that the United States made from selling the TOWs to Iran could be channeled to the needy contras. National Security Advisor John Poindexter, North's superior, approved the plan—although he insists he never informed President Reagan of the idea in an effort to shield him from its questionable legality. Casey loved the idea, appreciating the irony of using money gained from one enemy to help fight another.

The story of the arms-for-hostages deal first came to light in *Al-Shiraa*, a Lebanese magazine, on November 2, 1986. The first responses from the Reagan administration were noncommittal, mixed with anger; they didn't want the release of the remaining hostages to be fouled up. Eventually, though, the story did come out, and when the money trail was traced, it led to North's channeling of profits to the contras (as it turned out, because of some mix-up regarding Swiss bank account numbers, the contras never received all of the money they were supposed to get).

SCANDAL

The Iran-Contra scandal was only one of many that were linked to the CIA under Casey. The first scandal concerned Casey's appointment of Max Hugel, a friend and fellow Reagan campaigner, to the important post of head of Clandestine Services. Hugel wasn't in office long before he was forced out because of charges of illegal business practices. Casey himself narrowly survived two inquiries into his business and financial past. There was also the short-lived "Debategate" scandal. Casey is alleged to have aided in obtaining a copy of Jimmy Carter's debate strategy book during the 1980 presidential campaign. Nothing ever came of the charge.

The true scandals of Casey's years as DCI were bona fide spy scandals. The one that received the most press attention was the John Walker/Jerry Whitworth case. Spying for the Soviets, solely for the money and the thrill of it, Walker enlisted the help of other members of his family and of his friend Whitworth. The most damaging bit of espionage they did was to give away key encryption material, detailing certain Navy codes and ciphers. While this was a nasty blow during peacetime, it would have been devastating during a war. The KGB case officers for the Walker spy ring were treated like heroes in the Soviet Union; one was named Hero of the Soviet Union; two others received the Order of the Red Banner.

Another scandal concerned the defection of Vitaly Yurchenko of the KGB. When Yurchenko defected in the summer of 1985, it was initially regarded as quite a coup—Yurchenko was a high-level KGB officer, with 25 years of experience. One night at a restaurant in Georgetown, however, Yurchenko got up from his table and never came back. He returned to the Soviet Union. Casey was accused of bungling the matter, but he shrugged it off as mishandling. Indeed, many who "cross over" do often come down with a case of "defector blues." Suddenly cut off from all they know and love, in a country where no one speaks their language, some do return home. Besides, Yurchenko did reveal an important piece of intelligence before he left: He told them of a traitor spy who had done terrible damage.

Edward Lee Howard joined the CIA in 1981 at the age of 29. He was assigned to the Soviet Division. He was to go undercover to Moscow, one of the elite jobs in the agency. Because of restraints imposed by the Soviets, the CIA's Moscow station has to be small, and therefore, exceptionally hardworking. Because of its small size it can't afford to compartmentalize, and everyone must be able to do everyone else's job. The need-to-know doctrine is ignored and everyone knows everything. For this reason, Howard was trained in all capacities and was brought up to speed. In early 1983, however, before he was to leave for Moscow, he was given a lie detector test. Bad news. The polygraph indicated that he was drinking heavily, womanizing, using drugs and engaging in petty theft—all obvious security liabilities. He was fired.

About a year before, however, while Howard was being trained, things had begun to go terribly wrong at the Moscow station. Intelligence sources were drying up. In the worst episode, the case officer of Adolf Tolkachev, a physicist who provided highly sensitive information on radar and stealth technology, was exposed as a spy and expelled. Soon after that, Tolkachev disappeared and was presumably executed. Eventually, the entire Moscow station was virtually shut down.

Yurchenko had pointed his finger at Howard, who by this time was long gone from the CIA. The FBI tracked Howard down in New Mexico, but he eluded capture and eventually turned up in the Soviet Union.

Another destructive spy scandal involved not the CIA but the NSA—the National Security Agency, the agency responsible for intercepting the communications and breaking the codes of other countries. An NSA employee, Ronald

Official CIA photo portrait of William Casey, President Reagan's DCI for most of his two terms. [Credit: Courtesy of the Central Intelligence Agency]

Pelton, had given away one of the most important intercept operations the United States had. Code-named "Ivy Bells," it involved placing pods over Soviet underwater cables. These pods were undetectable electronically, and if the Soviets pulled up a cable to examine it, the pod would fall off. Although the operation was risky and dangerous—sending divers down to great depths in frigid Arctic waters to place the pods, and later, to retrieve tapes—it was worth it. The chief value of Ivy Bells was that the Soviets presumed that their cables were secure so often the messages that went back and forth on them were uncoded. Ivy Bells was begun when Stansfield Turner was DCI and Bobby Ray Inman was head of the NSA. It lasted until 1981 when the Soviets, informed by Pelton, zeroed in on the pods and removed them. Pelton is now in prison serving a sentence of three consecutive life terms plus 10 years.

One other spy scandal during Casey's watch showed how friends often spy on friends. Jonathan Jay Pollard of the Naval Investigative Service was convicted of spying for the Israelis.

There were also a couple of scandals that came to light shortly after Casey stepped down as DCI. Both involved the U.S. embassy in Moscow. First it was discovered that the new chancery that the United States had built to expand the old embassy was riddled with Soviet listening devices. Some were so incredibly sophisticated—cavities in the I-beams of the building that would resonate to the sound of human speech—and so hard to detect that the building would either have to be torn down or completely overhauled, at a cost of hundreds of millions of dollars. It was also revealed in the spring of 1987 that at least one Marine guard at the embassy had been seduced by female KGB agents into allowing them access to classified areas.

Of all the scandals that rocked the Reagan administration, however, none was as important as the Iran-contra affair. Casey and the CIA were never the primary focus of the scandal. That honor fell to North and others, and to the question of what President Reagan knew and when. Still, Casey and his agency were involved most of the way. In June 1988, the CIA station chief in Costa Rica at the time of the illegal arms shipments to the contras was implicated in the affair. Joseph Fernandez, who used the name "Tomas Castillo" for the illegal transactions, thus became the first CIA officer to be officially charged with involvement.

On December 15, 1986, Casey suffered a seizure and was rushed to the hospital. Deputy Director Robert Gates took over as DCI. Six weeks later, after improving considerably, Casey was visited by Gates. He told Gates that he thought it was "time for me to get out of the way." The next day he tendered his resignation, six years and one day after he was sworn in as DCI. He died on May 6, 1987, the day after Congress began public hearings into the Iran-contra affair.

LOOKING AHEAD

Traditionally, the deputy director does not rise to become DCI (only Dulles and Helms have done so), and Gates was no exception. The DCI appointed after Casey was Judge William Webster, who had been head of the FBI. He was sworn in on May 26, 1987. It was the first time that anyone had ever made such a jump between the two agencies. As for the other major positions at the agency, Gates resumed his position as deputy director, and Richard Stolz was appointed the new deputy director of operations, the chief of Clandestine Services.

With the election of George Bush to the presidency in November 1988—the first head of intelligence to be elected president—there was a great deal of speculation concerning Webster's future as DCI. As is customary with any change of administration, top officials submit their resignations to the president-elect; he then has the option of accepting or refusing the resignations. Bush recently announced that Webster would be staying on.

Current Director of Central Intelligence William H. Webster is the first DCI to have also been the head of the FBI. [Credit: Courtesy of the Central Intelligence Agency]

Webster was appointed to bring stability to the agency, reeling from the turmoil of its involvement in the Iran-Contra scandal, and by all accounts Webster did create that stability. He punished those in the agency who were involved in the Iran-Contra affair and he forged much better relations between the agency and Congress, strictly abiding by the rules set up to let the Congressional Oversight committee watch over covert actions. Further, his tenure as DCI so far has been marked by a distinctive shift from the path Casey embarked on. Webster did not want to become a policymaker as Casey did and he did not think the DCI should have a place in the cabinet. Webster felt, as George Bush himself stated in his book, *Looking Forward*, that the DCI should be solely an advisor and that, in fact, he "should go out of his way to avoid even the appearance of getting involved in policy-making."

But Webster has not been without his critics, a score of intelligence veterans, most of whom served with Clandestine Services. They think that Webster has been too cautious, too rule-bound, when it comes to covert actions. They also think he was too vigorous in ousting those who were involved in the Iran-Contra scandal.

Whatever the ultimate verdict on Webster's tenure, it is certain that he will have to address the concerns raised in "Intelligence Requirements for the 1990s," a report released in November 1988 by the Consortium for the Study of Intelligence, a privately funded public interest group. The report was endorsed by such varied intelligence experts as former president Richard Nixon, the chairman of the Senate Select Committee on Intelligence, and one of the possible choices for DCI, Brent Scowcroft. The report indicates that the intelligence community's technical means for intelligence gathering—the spy planes and satellites, the eavesdropping devices, etc—are fine, but that the human resources need replenishing. The United States needs more and more specialized spies. The report also highlighted the need for improved counterintelligence coordination, citing the Robert Lee Howard spy scandal as an example of what happens when the CIA and FBI aren't communicating.

And, of course, the report calls for increased covert action. Covert action is what the CIA has become known for, even though that's not really what it was mandated to do. As ineffective and embarrassing as covert action has often proven to be it is nonetheless very enticing. For presidents and their advisors it has always held out, and always will hold out, the promise of doing things quickly and quietly. As Richard Helms once noted: "Covert action is like a damn good drug. It works, but if you take too much of it, it will kill you." Only time will tell how the U.S. government in general and the CIA in particular are faring with their particular drug addiction.

GLOSSARY

Bay of Pigs   The CIA's unsuccessful attempt in
                          April 1961 to invade Cuba with an
                          army of Cuban exiles at the Bay of
                          Pigs.

CIG   The Central Intelligence Group.
                          The CIA's immediate predecessor
                          as America's intelligence agency.

cipher   Ciphers are used to scramble and
                          hide the meaning of a message so
                          that only a person who knows the
                          cipher can decode the message.

clandestine   Secret, or hidden. Spies work in a
                          clandestine manner.

Clandestine Services The common name at the CIA for
                          the Directorate of Operations,
                          which carries out the CIA's most

secret and most sensitive operations.

Cold War
The name given to the ongoing conflict between the United States and the Soviet Union. A war involving soldiers and guns is a "hot" war; therefore, this conflict between the United States and the Soviet Union and involving statesmen and spies is a "cold" war.

contras
The forces fighting against the Sandinista regime in Nicaragua.

Communist Party
The one political party in the Soviet Union, built on the principles put forward by Karl Marx and V.I. Lenin. There are other communist parties in other countries, but this is *the* Communist Party.

counterintelligence
The field of endeavor that seeks to block and counter the intelligence gathering activities of other nations.

covert action
Spy operations that are carried out under cover without any public knowledge. They are usually intended to influence the course of events in other nations.

CTs
Career trainees at the CIA.

DCI
Director of central intelligence —the head of the CIA.

DDCI   Deputy director of central intelli-
                    gence—the number-two spot at the
                    CIA.

DDO   Deputy director of operations—the
                    head of the Directorate of Opera-
                    tions (Clandestine Services).

disinformation False stories and half-truths that are
                    circulated to bolster a nation's
                    position.

Eastern bloc   Those communist European
                    nations that are strongly guided and
                    influenced by the Soviet Union.
                    Also known as the Soviet bloc or
                    the Warsaw Pact nations.

encryption   The act of scrambling a message
                    using a cipher.

Executive Action A small, short-lived group within
                    the CIA created to carry out assassi-
                    nations.

HUMINT   HUMan INTelligence—intelli-
                    gence gathered by agents and in-
                    formers as opposed to technically
                    gathered information.

infiltration   Getting an agent into another na-
                    tion, specifically a nation's govern-
                    ment, scientific circles or spy
                    service.

Iron Curtain   The line separating Western Europe
                    from Eastern Europe. The coun-
                    tries of the Eastern bloc are "behind
                    the Iron Curtain."

junta

A governing body, usually military, that runs a country after suddenly overthrowing the previous regime.

KGB

Committee for State Security (Komitet Gosudarstvennoy Bezopastnosti)—the Soviet Union's spy service.

left-wing

Strongly liberal, with an emphasis on liberty, human rights and the need for all people to take responsibility for each other.

Mafia

A generic name given to organized crime in the United States.

Marxism

The political theory based on the writings of Karl Marx. He advocated a state system without private ownership of goods or of industry, where everything is owned by all the people through their government.

Nazism

The National Socialist movement in Germany led by Adolf Hitler, which prescribed strict order and governmental control of all things, and the elimination of all those who didn't fit the Nazi racial mold, especially Jews.

NRO

National Reconnaissance Office. Part of Air Force Intelligence, it operates the spy satellites.

NSC   National Security Council. The group that assesses the U.S. security situation and formulates the highest and most sensitive level of foreign policy.

OPC   Office of Policy Coordination. The first postwar covert action group of the United States.

Operation Mongoose   The CIA's post-Bay of Pigs operation to eliminate Castro and topple the communist regime in Cuba.

OSO   Office of Special Operations. The CIA's first covert action group.

OSS   Office of Strategic Services. The U.S. intelligence service during World War II.

Pentagon   The huge, five-sided (hence its name) building in Washington, D.C., which houses the Department of Defense.

Phoenix program   The CIA operation during the war in Vietnam that aimed to eliminate the enemy's leadership through assassination and intimidation.

propaganda   Information and ideas circulated to bolster a nation's position and to put it in the best possible light.

reconnaissance   Scouting out the enemy's territory and reporting back with the information.

right-wing　　　　　Strongly conservative, with an emphasis on order, control (including the suppression of human rights when necessary), limited governmental interference and individual responsibility for one's welfare.

Sandinistas　　　　The communist revolutionary government that seized power in Nicaragua in 1979. It is named in honor of a rebel leader, Augusto Sandino, who was killed in 1934.

secret police　　　A security force used by a government to suppress its political opponents.

SPG　　　　　　　Special Procedures Group. The CIA group set up to influence the Italian elections in 1948.

station chief　　　The CIA's chief in a country or region where the agency has a full-scale operation, or station, running. The station chief often has a cover job with a U.S. embassy or consulate.

spy tech　　　　　The technology used in gathering intelligence.

Technical Services Division　　The division within the CIA that produces the technology, such as listening devices and explosives, used in espionage.

totalitarianism   Total government control over the
                             lives of citizens.

U-2   A spy plane. Gary Powers was
                             flying a U-2 in May 1960 when he
                             was shot down over the Soviet
                             Union.

SUGGESTED READING

Agee, Philip. *Inside the Company: The CIA Diary.* New York: Penguin Books, 1975.

Bledowska, Celina, and Bloch, Jonathan. *KGB/CIA.* New York: Exeter Books, 1987.

Corson, William R. *The Armies of Ignorance.* New York: Dial Press, 1977.

Dulles, Allen Welsh. *The Craft of Intelligence.* New York: Harper and Row, 1963.

Knightley, Phillip. *The Second Oldest Profession.* New York: W.W. Norton and Company, 1986.

Marchetti, Victor, and Marks, John D. *The CIA and the Cult of Intelligence.* New York: Laurel, 1980.

Martin, David C. *Wilderness of Mirrors.* New York: Ballantine Books, 1981.

Powers, Thomas. *The Man Who Kept the Secrets: Richard Helms and the CIA.* New York: Alfred A. Knopf, 1979.

Snepp, Frank. *Decent Interval.* New York: Random House, 1977.

Wise, David, and Ross, Thomas B. *The Espionage Establishment.* New York: Random House, 1967.

Woodward, Bob. *Veil: The Secret Wars of the CIA 1981-1987.* New York: Simon and Schuster, 1987.

Yost, Graham. *Spy Tech.* New York: Facts On File, 1985.

INDEX

327.1   Yost, Graham
YoS
          The CIA